Leather and Lace

A BOOK OF POETRY

BY

LEONA FAYE HORATH

RoseDog Books

PITTSBURGH, PENNSYLVANIA 15238

RoseDog Books
585 Alpha Drive
Suite 103
Pittsburgh, PA 15238
Visit our website at *www.rosedogbookstore.com*

ISBN: 978-1-4809-6783-0
eISBN 978-1-4809-6760-1

Contents

COUNT YOUR BLESSINGS 1

VIRTUE 2

THE LAST ROSE 3

MY BLESSINGS TO GARRY CUSHMAN 4

WITHOUT YOU 5

WALLS 6

DAD 7

TO A FLICKER 8

THE SACRED DOVE 9

TRUST IN GOD 10

BECAUSE OF YOU MOTHER —
   TO MY MOTHER, JUNE, AND PAT .11

THE FLOWER 12

CARLE NURSES
   DEDICATED TO NURSES AT CARLE IN CHAMPAIGN, IL .13

WINDOWS 14

ALMOST FINE 15

FAITH 16

BLUE HEAVEN 17

REMEMBERING HIM 18

FREE WILL 19

TO QUIET INSPIRATION 20

MY LOVE 21

SET FREE 22

RAINBOWS 23

A COLD HEART 24

"IF ONLY" 25

LOVING HIM 26

TRUST IN GOD 27

WORDS 28

TRUE LOVE 29

EMPTY 30

NO MORE VACANCY 31

A LIGHTER LOAD 32

MY SPECIAL FRIEND 33

DREAM OF HEAVEN 34

VOICES DEDICATED TO MY OLDEST SON,
    MICHAEL DAVID VAN MATRE, JR. 35
THE PANDORA'S BOX 36
MY SWEET FRIEND 37
A LOAD TO SHARE 38
THE GIFT TO MY SON, TIM MATLOCK 39
NO ONE SAID LIFE WAS EASY 40
FRIENDSHIP 41
ANY WAY 42
DARK BLACK PAIN 43
LAZY DAISY 44
AFTER THE RAIN 45
I LIKE IT WHEN IT RAINS 46
EMPTY PROMISES 47
A DISGRACE CALLED WAR 48
LITTLE ANGELS 49
THINGS I CHERISH 50
DREAMS ARE REAL 51
IN THE PRESENT DAY 52
IT'S YOUR CHOICE 53
LIVING IN THE LIGHT 54
LOLLIPOPS 55
PEARLS 56
INTO THE WIND 57
AS THYSELF 58
TAINTED LOVE 59
JADER 60
AFTER THE RAIN 61
THE DANCE 62
COLTON 63
TOUGH TIMES 64
COURAGE 65
THE SHOOTING STAR 66
MY BLESSING 67
A TEACHER'S PRAYER 68
WHY COULDN'T I SEE? 69

MY HEAVENLY FATHER 70

DYING LOVE 71

KISS ME SOFTLY 72

ANGELS FROM ABOVE 73

SECOND FIDDLE 74

HEAVEN BOUND 75

NO MORE TEARS 76

MOTHER, BECAUSE OF YOU 77

MIRROR, MIRROR 78

MY BEST FRIEND 79

REMEMBER HIM 80

MY FRIEND, MOMMA 81

FAITH 82

LOVING LIFE 83

JOY 84

OUR HOME 85

MISSING YOU 86

SO SPECIAL 87

CHRISTMAS SCROOGE 88

A MOTHER'S LOVE 89

TRUST AND BELIEVE 90

MOANING SOULS 91

DEVILS TONGUE 92

A PRAYER TO ST. ANTHONY'S HOSPITAL 93

INNER PEACE 94

ONE OF A KIND 95

STOP AND SMELL THE ROSES 96

IN TIMES OF PRAYER 97

ALL ALONE 98

MISSING MOTHER 99

SILVER LINING 100

FADED LOVE 101

THINGS I ENJOY 102

TIME HEALS ALL WOUNDS 103

SHOOTING STAR 104

JESUS' BLESSING 105

THANKS DAD 106
MY LITTLE BUTTERFLY 107
DRAGONS 108
SUNFLOWERS 109
HEAVEN KNOWS 110
JESUS 111
LET JESUS INTO YOUR HEART 112
THE QUESTION OF LIFE 113
A PLACE IN HEAVEN 114
MY SAVIOR 115
COLOR 116
DEEP SCARS 117
NO HEART 118
A FOOL OUT OF ME 119
TODAY 120
A DARK STRANGER 121
NO FOOL 122
JUST ANOTHER DAY 123
DREAMS 124
HEAR ME NOW 125
HAVE FAITH 126
ISAIAH —- A DREAM COME TRUE 127
TELL MY HEART LIES 128
PEACE IN HEAVEN 129
FOLLOW JESUS 130
BUTTERFLIES 131
CHUCK-A-LUCK 132
THE WINTER OF MY LIFE .133
MY DAD 134
RELAX 135
A PRAYER FROM MOM 136
THE LOSS 137
TO DAD 138
MY BEST FRIEND 139
A MAN VERY LOVED 140
ECHOES 141

THE SPIRIT OF A CHILD 142
ILLUSIONS 143
TRUE LOVE 144
LOVING YOU 145
THE LIGHT 146
FINDING JESUS 147
WHERE ARE YOU? 148
CATCH ME 149
TRUST AND BELIEVE 150
HELP ME SAY GOOD-BY 151
THE ANGELS DANCE 512
MISSING YOU 153
THE GIFT 154
THE ANGEL 155
WE ARE WHAT WE THINK 156
FREEDOM 157
MICHAEL 158
THEY'LL NEVER BE ANOTHER YOU 159
FRIEND 160
MY DEAR MOTHER 161
HEROES 162
THE RIVER 163
I LIKE IT WHEN IT RAINS 164
MICHAEL DAVID 165
JESUS IS MY LIFE 166
MY FATHER 167
REMEMBERING HIM 168
MY SPECIAL FRIEND 169
CHEERS 170
ONE CHANCE 171
THE BIG CHANGE 172
CLOSE FRIENDS 173
A SPECIAL PLACE 174
TIME TO MEND 175
MY BLESSING 176
TIC TOC 177

LOVE EVERLASTING 178
HOW CAN I SAY GOOD-BY? 179
WENT AWAY 180
MY MICHAEL 181
ANGELA 182
GET IT DONE 183
CHILDREN 184
WHAT IS LIFE ALL ABOUT? 185
A BABE IN THE NIGHT 186
"FOR GOODNESS SAKE" 187
TIMOTHY 188
LEAN ON THE LORD 189
DEDICATED TO MY SIS, PRECIOUS PATTY 190
DEDICATED TO JAMES DILLOW .191
REONA IS HER NAME 192
ENJOY EACH DAY 193
CROSSROADS BANK 194
MY SWEET SISTER, LINDA 195
AN ANGEL THAT WE KNOW 196
FAITH WILL CARRY YOU THROUGH 197
LOVE 198
THE EAGLE 199
CLYDE'S DREAM 200
DEALING WITH CRIME 201

Count Your Blessings

We are all like little children and need to know we're loved.
To connect comes understanding and this is the most beloved.
We are all like little children to prove that we're the best.
Spending a lifetime collecting possessions until we're laid to rest.
We are all like little children and compare our tragic woes.
When we should be thinking of our blessings and counting them on our toes.
Beauty is like magic; it's here for just a while, and as it fades, it seeps inside
and stays for just a while.
So here me little children . . . Don't let life pass you by.
One day you learn to spell your name, the next you say goodbye.

Virtue

In this world our spirit is relieved by the enchantment of beauty, but our soul is restored only when truth and wisdom prevail.

We seek the warmth of the sun just as the flower flourishes in it's infinite radiance.

We desire many things, but need few.

If we are blessed with virtue, it grew from disparity and thrived . . .

In solemn unfaltering faith.

The Last Rose

I planted a garden that bloomed all summer long, and as I tended my garden, I sang a special song.

The roses became more fragrant as they blossomed past the fence. The stems were so thick that they would often pinch.

A wicker basket full to give to mother as she laid. She once was very healthy, but became very frayed.

I went into my garden, but little could I stay. Mother died three days ago and I felt so dismayed; because all the roses had turned brown except a special one that stayed.

I brought it to her graveside and laid it on her plot.

The song I used to sing in the garden, I sang on that spot.

As tears welled up inside my eyes, I knew God had a plan.

To save the very last rose for Mother as she walks in His promised land.

My Blessings to Garry Cushman

In every ones life there is someone whom God blesses to share love.
Knowing my need for someone strong, persistent, and full of love,
He gave me you.
Yesterday you gave me strength to live.
Today you give me persistence to cope.
Tomorrow I have the promise of love and a good reason to hope.
God has blessed my life with many things . . .
But best of all —- He gave me you.

> I love you so,
> Leona

Without You

Day break lights the window and the day is fresh and new; another day I'll have to face living without you.

I pour a cup of coffee where we used to sit and talk; but I can't take the pain I feel so I go for a walk.

I see the morning sunlight and hear the birds that sing; but I don't feel the same old joy that these things used to bring.

I think about you most the time, like you're engraved inside my mind. Yes, how am I going to make it without you.

The day is long and empty and I dread the thought of night. I'm used to holding you so close when everything was right.

I say a prayer that you'll be back, as I hang my coat upon the rack and wipe away the tears that fill my eyes.

I wonder if you think of me or is our love just history, I have so many things I have to say.

If I tried to call you on the phone, would you tell me please what went wrong? Is there something I can say to change your mind?

I think about you most of the time like you're engraved inside my mind.

How am I going to make it without you?

Walls

Hear me now, before the night rides in and gathers the empty shadows. They are all faded together in hues of desperate grays.

They slide slowly down these painted walls, only to taunt me until dawn.

Walls that grow smaller.

Walls that grow colder.

They sigh as they hold in all my pain. Hear me now for tomorrow may be too late. As I cry out into the darkness, I fear they shall consume me before the night is gone.

Hear me now. Please hear me now.

Walls that grow older.

Walls that may smolder as the pain becomes stronger . . . until the night becomes longer and one time morning may never come.

Hear me now,

please!

Hear me now . . .

Dad

Here is nine smiling faces, and time never erases the love and wisdom we learned from you.

As we grew up, others became more aware that you taught us to care, to love, and to share.

Now that we are all grown with many children of our own . . . We can handle responsibility because of what you have shown, and we want our children to learn virtues we have learned from you.

When we thank the Lord for all our blessings, you are definitely included for sure in there, too.

To a Flicker

Black isn't always a color, sometimes it's a feeling.

Deep down in the depths of my innermost soul . . . my life light is flickering.

Along with each broken promise, heartache, and lost dream, I have also lost my smile.

Everyday soon becomes . . . Just another day.

. . . Just another day.

The sun can no longer warm places it can't reach.

I feel dark inside like the midnight loneliness of a lost love.

Inside, my life light is flickering.

By the way, if the light goes out, does anyone, please have a match?

The Sacred Dove

Love is like a sacred dove that comes and sits softly on your shoulder.
Beckon it not to always be.
Love comes with no promises or commitments.
For if you try to capture love,
It will
  wither
    . . . like the rose.

Trust in God

With folded hands and tearful eyes; I say a prayer to thee for
God has given me many things that bring joy and love to me.
    Though life is sometimes hard to bear and things don't work our so
well; I thank the Lord for all He's done to help me when I fail.
    So put your faith in the one above. He'll help you find your way.
    For if you've got your trust in God; you'll never go astray.

Because of You Mother -

Because of you I have found a friend that is always there when I can' t go on.

You make me feel loved and part of your family, because of this, I belong.

Because of you I learned to trust, just when everyone else did me wrong. Before I've been so hurt, I feel nothing but blue.

You've been by my side through the sunshine and the rain. We've shared the tears of both laughter and pain.

I'll never be able to repay you for what you're done for me. You took me out of the darkness, let go, then set me free.

Because of you —- now I've learned to love myself and be the best that I can be.

When I was blinded by remorse, you helped me see. Life can be both good and bad and I need to do what's right for me.

We've shared both the laughter and then other times toward each other we'd be mad.

Then in a few days we'll make up because we are sad.

My memory of you makes me smile because you always went the extra mile.

All I can do is say "thank you" for what you've done for me. You've always been my friend and let me be me.

The Flower

The flower is a symbol of love, so delicately handcrafted from our precious God above.

A rainbow of bright colors, both tall and small. Their beauty admired and simply enjoyed by all.

They lean toward the sunshine and soak up summer rain. They are given to friends and loved ones both in times of joy and pain.

The flower is carried by the smiling bride in a gorgeous white veil and dress; and laid up on our graveside with tears, when we're laid to rest.

Take time to enjoy their beauty and share them with a special friend.

They'll hold dear this thoughtful gift and all the love it sends.

I'll forever cherish flowers because they bring smiles all year through.

If I give you a flower, will you give me one too?

Carle Nurses

Dedicated to Nurses at Carle in Champaign, IL

They give all they can and walk twenty miles each day.

But you know what; they wouldn't have it any other way.

They are dedicated and sharing and with eyes so beautiful, so very caring.

God blessed them with a talent that I call very valiant and the nurses always make you glad you chose to be here.

Their smiles are plenty and no amount of money could replace the nurses at Carle.

So, if you're sick or need surgery, they treat you like a rose in deep burgundy.

Words can't express how much they care. They have smiling faces and time never erases seeing them walk their twenty miles.

Windows

Lord, please give me one day of peace.

Stop the madness and make the panic cease. I'm tired of being a recluse in my own home. I'm tired of the torment and being so alone.

I look out the window and watch as the world goes by.

I can't take it much longer and all I do is cry. Lord, I need a miracle to set me free. I can't be what I need and want to be.

It's hard to answer the phone or a knock on the door.

Lord, I just can't live like this any more.

Yes Lord, I need a miracle to set me free. I'd worship you forever just wait and see.

I want to be like I was before. Please help me not to be afraid, God, when I walk out the door.

Almost Fine

What is it you're thinking of when you gaze into blank space and leave me quietly behind —- to watch you until you return.

Where is it that you go to as I see you sit in the dark with your drink and watch your cigarette burn?

Have I lost you already just when I thought we had found each other?

Please, please, don't tell me now —- maybe tomorrow I can handle the pain. Then I'll pick up the pieces of my broken heart and cry as I walk in the rain.

I want you to hold and rock me as I pardon my self and try to keep from going insane.

Where can I find the map so I can travel back inside you?

I used to make you laugh so hard and we'd stay up talking by candlelight until dawn.

I thought everything was fine, but you slipped away from me ever so slowly until I was gone.

—- Gone from that special place you tucked people you loved —- but where do you put them when you're done?

I have so many feelings and I can't describe all turning and twisting inside, that I want to run.

I took you to be with me forever, but in just a few —- years it's gone. It seems like we've only just begun.

I won't hold you back if you want to leave, but keep the door open just in case —-

In case you change your mind.

When you go I'll watch you slowly walk away into the night breeze.

Good-bye my love. I whisper, and take care. I'm not going anywhere except to bed and hold your pillow and cry. So don't look back if you'd be so kind.

Good-bye my love —- good-bye.

As you fade into the night, I gently close the door and take a very long, deep breath.

It's going to be hard and it will take a lot of time —- but someday I'll be almost fine.

Faith

When I am in deep despair and can't find hope anywhere, I have to remember times from the past when I felt the same, and this, too, won't last.

I think of my life from the past and now, and how God gave me faith and strength to endure and outlast.

God gave me hope to hang tight on the rope and even more when I found it very hard to cope.

So remember the sun is shining bright behind the dark gloomy sky.

We all have to keep on trying and not question why.

So hold on to our faith and all you have to do is try.

Blue Heaven

To die from a life of sorrow, pain, and agony is the only way to set us free.

Dying is done once and is all planned in our destiny; as well as our faith, and trust, and also hope, for all our lives and for a future place I call Blue Heaven is a God send —- So, I have to do it all just right.

I will not give up the fight. This journey called life is not a dress rehearsal. This is not; it lasts as long as a very short commercial.

I wish everyone would believe this way. We are like a very grain of sand on a big and long, beautiful and peaceful place called Blue Heaven.

Remembering Him

When you're wishing on a shining star, always keep your faith and if He's willing, you're go far,

Far and near, He's the best for you, forget about the rest. Loving Him will warm your soul —- especially when the adversity in life takes its toll.

Keep in mind that He's yesterday, today, and tomorrow —- and will always be your companion in sickness, pain, and sorrow.

It's His Blue Heaven and earth —- we're just here for the ride.

A ride to Heaven if you keep His promises and do God's will. Just believe and be silent and listen to the still.

Leona

Free Will

Just like the birds that fly so carefree in the sunny sky —-

Be also like the little birds and never ask why. What good is faith if you don't really believe or try ?

Surrender your life to Him and you have to believe. He'll give you so much more, please think twice before you decide to leave —- to do it alone is too much of a chore.

He gives us free will to love and worship Him in many different ways.

Just believe in Him and trust and He'll be by your side —- remember this.

To Quiet Inspiration

I long for quiet hills; secluded between daybreak and sunset
—- Below a million stars and where time is never an issue.
To feel comfort from the sounds of nature.
—-Where peace and nature capture me.
I'm entwined with much needed solitude and appreciation for the simple life.
—- To renew my spirit, body and mind.
I have to feel captured by the tranquility and at the same time let go and become one with everything around me.
Serenity is God's gift to us.
The quiet hills wait for me patiently and know I will return.
—- will enjoy and leave again to do God's will.
Such as nature and the hills do theirs.
Take time to appreciate God's gifts.
Some call nature's heaven. I call it my sanctuary and refuge.
I need to go again where there is peace and solitude.
Where I can give thanks for our gifts of peace from nature.
The hills wait for me.

My Love

Your love for me shows in your eyes.
You have the heart of hearts, it tells no lies.
I will love you until the day I die,
—- Then I'll meet you, my love, beyond blue skies.

Leona

Set Free

I was a butterfly trapped in a cage.
I knew I was a lot like momma from an early age.
She also loved butterflies and wanted to be set free.
I was like momma and wished this also for me.
We were like everyone else — but to a certain degree.
But momma said it's OK to be different or unique like me.
To be yourself is a gift you see.
I always loved momma and best of all I learned it's OK to be different and I also loved me.

Leona

Rainbows

Don't cry for Gerald —- he's in a better place.

Just hold onto the cherished memories you shared that time can never erase. Remember his smile, his laughter, and the way he walked and talked; and when he'd get mad, hid, clam up, and balked.

Gerald will never again drive to St. Louis to be a painter all day long. God promoted him to master painter and this is where he belongs.

When you see a beautiful sunset with hues of orange and purple haze —- or gorgeous rainbows fill the heavens and he paints the sky in colors just for you and me.

So if you're down and out and feel empty and blue —- go outside and watch the sunset change from orange to purple hues.

If you feel something drop upon your head, it's probably paint from Gerald's brush as he changes the sunset from purple to gorgeous orange and red.

Look up and he might smile back and wave; he'll take the time you know.

Yes, Cush is now the master painter and he had to go farther than St. Louis to get this job.

A Cold Heart

A   There are quiet places in hearts and faces where they no longer feel.

There are puddles of tears after all the years of hurt and sorrow —- Not even wanting to see another tomorrow. It will be all the same, nothing will change.

Eyes that search
Hands that reach out
But I've learned to let go, heaven knows.

I see what really is but still I can't believe that he's so cold and selfish and I asked him to leave.

Vanity is his crime in later years —- he'll do his time.

When he gets old, no one will be around. Everyone stayed away because he had no heart they found.

Eyes that search
Hands that reach out
And still know it's
Best for me to let go.

What really is will be. Things will never change and I have to do what's best for me. He hasn't learned you have to give to receive.

With God's help I'll heal my heart and mind. I gave him all my love and time. There is no more that I can give. So I have to leave him. I resign.

Eyes that search
Hands that reach out

The reasons for the breakup has been truly clear.

I can almost smile once again and no longer cry. He's out of my life and I know exactly why.

Now, I don't feel like I want to cry.
Now, I don't feel like I want to die.

"If Only"

Listen to the silence and feel the quiet breeze.

No sounds of violence to interrupt while the whole world sleeps.

If only we could always live where love and companionships were normal to give.

Just imagine how much better the world would be for all to live, see, and best of all, be free.

Loving Him

Sometimes life just doesn't seem fair.

Everything can be against you. It seems like there's no hope; only lonely despair.

Always remember that He is on your side. I, myself, have been down many a rocky road. I have come to the end of many roads a stronger more compassionate person.

He is with you and can feel every tear you cry.

Both through the sunshine and the high tide, He will never leave your side.

Hold onto your faith and don't let go because soon the sun will warm your heart and you will smile again.

Remember to always love Him because "He loved you first".

Trust in God

With folded hands and tearful eyes I say a prayer to thee. For God has given many things that bring joy and love to me.

Though life is sometimes hard to bear and things don't go so well.

I thank God for all He's done to help me when I fail.

It's hard sometimes to see the right when everything goes wrong.

But the pain in life is just like love, they both are very strong.

So, put your faith in the one above. He'll help you find your way. For if you've got your trust in God, you'll never go astray.

Words

Words are like a paint brush .

They can instill feeling to the heart, like color on a canvas.

Each work should be as painstakingly chosen as the artist chooses his palette —- to create a vision of hope and thought; to stir the human emotion.

A writer has the ability to touch the very soul of mankind.

May it be done ever so gently. Maybe just a nudge to their heart will fire the passion in life again.

For a life without feeling contains as much beauty as a rainbow without color.

True Love

It is true in love, the same as in freedom of spirit, that when it is given in namesake only, it is like the dove.

It comes and sits softly on your shoulder —- beckon it not to promise you it will always be.

Love comes with no promises or commitments. If you try to capture love, it will wither like the rose.

Empty

Words are left unspoken like unmade beds.

People grasps on to one another but feel nothing in their hands.

Their emptiness is consumed with more sorrow —- but at least it can cry.

Empty is like a vacancy that eats at your insides like leeches.

Sometimes I fee like I've died many times before. But yet, I continue only because that's all I know how to do.

Empty is a feeling I sleep with when the night is cold and nobody is there to hold me when I cry.

No More Vacancy

Your eyes are like a vacant home.
One can tell even from a distance that no one lives there.
If you let God move inside your heart;
—- the world will feel like your neighbor
—- the view will be peaceful
—- and best of all, your foundation will always be strong.

A Lighter Load

Life would be so hard to bear if in your heart no love was there.

God gave us love so we could care.

He gave us joy, happiness, and love to share.

The pain in life is sure to be a lighter load to bear by knowing you have friends who care and our Lord who is always there.

My Special Friend

When I have dark and empty days and my future seems but just a haze;
I have a friend who knows just what to say or not to talk at all.
Sometimes, when I've had it over my head with problems,
I can't seem to shed. My friend is right there sharing life's burdens
with me.
She can always make me laugh even when I had forgotten how to.
Through the years, sharing both the laughter and the tears; my heart
holds this person very dear.
She always believed in me even when I stopped believing in myself.
God has blessed my life in many special ways.
Having a best friend who is also my sister is twice as special to me.

Dedicated to all my sisters

Dream of Heaven

It is when I awake that the chaos begins. I feel and see a nightmare, but am wide awake.

Only in my dreams do I descend and escape for a while.

My soul goes beyond what one can see and touch.

Finding peace and solace somewhere in a place I'd like to go.

I see the world full of chaos and confusion.

People crying out for help, yet only scurrying about faster to run from what they know is true.

I hurt for them just as I hurt for myself.

Wishing I could end their pain like me, too.

We suffer each day as we walk through this journey called life.

I look forward to the peace Jesus promises me.

I close my eyes and dream of heaven.

Voices

Dedicated to my OLDEST son,
Michael David van Matre, Jr.

He can hear them whispering when he's all alone.

Voices echo into the night with a low-pitched tone.

As he tries to sleep they taunt him and he screams Jesus please, "Stop the madness and make the voices cease."

He said, "everyone has their limit,

I believe I've crossed the line."

He tried to drown out the voices, but their noise remained. Raising his emotions —- trying to drive him insane.

Another night without sleep.

His anger is running steep.

He makes a pot of coffee as Randy Travis sings his favorite songs.

Sipping on the coffee, tears begin to flow. The anguish he goes through —- no one would even know.

"Please my precious Jesus, take the voices away. It's 9:00 a.m. —- three days awake. He wonders how much more he can take.

With trembling hands, he takes his pills and shivers as he gets a chill.

He opens the blinds and watches as the rain comes pouring down.

Who needs sunshine anyway when no one else ever comes around —- but voices.

The Pandora's Box

I cry out in the darkness and echos of my pain go unheard.

Only the sound of tears I can no longer hide cautiously gather and pool around my feet.

For way too long this pain I feel went undenied. It was pushed down deep within my being and stuffed so much I wanted to die.

I told myself I had no time for its existence. I had to always be strong.

As time passed, the more pain I pushed down the stronger it grew.

I could no longer contain the gnarling beast that demanded to be heard!! Pain, anger, anguish and hurt seeped from the lid and grabbled me by the throat.

I could not breathe and I knew I had to leave.

So I began to pray, I asked God to forgive me of my sins and to destroy the ugly feeling I had trapped within the box.

After a few minutes, it stopped and I felt like a new person without the old baggage I carried around for years.

My Sweet Friend

Please hold me while I cry; if you don't mind.

Don't ask the reasons why I'm so hurt though right now I wish I could die.

I just can't hold back the tears, so much hurt and pain I wish I could disappear.

If you just be still and listen later on you can hear the stars in heaven glisten

Then I'll be forever grateful to the one who held me while I cried and never asked why the stars did glisten and then He disappeared into the heavens. Never did I see him again.

Load to Share

Life would be so hard to bear if in your heart no love was there.
God gave us love so we could care.
He gave us joy, happiness and love to share.
If you have friends who care, and our Lord who is always there, life is sure to be a lighter load to share and to bear.

The Gift to My Son, Tim Matlock

As you go off to train for war.

I will pray God keeps you safe here or maybe later on a distant shore.

Each night, as you lay your tired head down to sleep,

You're not alone son; you're not alone son. God will give you peace.

Be strong and brave, you're doing what's right.

Remember this in the battlefield when the enemy is close in sight.

If you get scared, get a grip and show your strength hasn't ripped.

Doing what is necessary even though you're afraid is what courage is all about.

I'm proud to be your Mother and more proud that you're my son.

You always stood your ground, and when looking for justice, searched until it was found.

We have to sacrifice our time and sometimes our lives are on the line; but freedom's a gift to all of us given by brave men and women who sacrifice and even precious sons like you.

Thank you, Tim, for your dedication and sacrifice so that we may share the gift.

I'm proud of you and thank you for fighting for my freedom.

> I'll always love and respect you,
> Mom

No One Said Life Was Easy

It takes time for people to grow.
It takes time for people to mend.
Seems you get through a major crisis and it starts all over again.
We get stronger as we endure life's pain longer.
It takes time for people to grow.
It takes time for people to mend.
Keep the faith and persevere; God will keep you strong 'till the very end.

Friendship

I have someone I can talk to and tell my secrets and even bare my soul.
I feel such comfort in her company when life has taken its toll.
We laugh at ourselves and trust with no boundaries.
When I hear the word friendship, I think of her.
Just wanted to let her know that I love her so and she is so very important
to me.

Any Way

If only love would wither up and blow away when a relationship is over and just thrown into the wind.

There would be so much less pain and sorrow to drag out tomorrow and a lot easier to make a fresh start.

Broken hearts never mend. They just hide inside behind a heart that is broken and a smile you can tell is not real.

The mirror will soon show the effects of being stripped of your pride.

It would be easier of you could have just died. Now your pride feels stripped and your heart has a wall-to-wall rip.

The emptiness pools up and comes streaming from dark despairing eyes any way.

Dark Black Pain

Sorrow has built a gate between you and me.

I see how strong you pain is when you look at me.

It's not so much the flood of tears always streaming down your face . . .

But the feel of black emptiness that surrounds your space.

I reach out and grab your ice-cold hand. Don't you know baby, I'm so scared of loosing you my man.

I'm trying so hard to understand. Please, for God's sake, let me in because I care. Give me your burdens because so much I care.

Your smile is lost in a pit of gloom. Your smile my dear used to light the room.

Each day I see you slip more away, I see you suffer in a dark cloud of hell.

I'm exhausted from praying that you'll soon be well.

Without you I feel lose in space. I long to see your beautiful smile on your face.

Together, we can be a strong pillar of one, but without your love, I no longer feel strong.

Get well my love. I've done all I can do. I have to save myself and I pray you'll be saved too.

Give me a few days. I've got to rest, "and you're my man – better be trying your best."

Lazy Daisy

Lazy Daisy had a big broad behind and wore wrinkled skirts of yellow and purple paisley and thought she looked fine.

She also wore big straw hats in the summer that shaded her big green eyes.

Many people in town considered Lazy Daisy the town nut case.

She never worked and spent all her time alone.

She had no computer, T.V. or even a telephone.

What did Lazy Daisy do all day with her time that made her big green eyes shine. She was the best writer from all around and wrote a lot of poetry and it all rhymed.

So she finished her book. Many years it took, but it hit three times on the best seller list.

She then lost more than 100 lbs. and all of a sudden everyone wanted to talk to Lazy Daisy.

She just smiled and went her merry way and said she was too busy and would talk to them another day.

So be careful who you laugh at; the laugh may be on you.

I was once a Lazy Daisy; how about you?

After the Rain

Too many major problems, and too many years of tears.
I feel overwhelmed and paralyzed by pain, worry, and fear.
I've prayed to God to help me, to give me hope to see.
Someday all this too will pass and I'll feel peace inside of me.
I have to remember to take one day at a time.
Storms don't last forever, and once again, the sun will shine.
My faith I must lean on and is the most important thing in my life.
I have faith that God will be with me through both the sunshine and the strife.

I Like It When It Rains

Dark clouds gather over the little creek and pond up the road.

I can hear a symphony of crickets in tune and I'm sure it's a trio of big full frogs looking cool in their new togs.

The trees of gold and yellow look bright against the dark blue sky. The tops of the trees are swaying and a whirlwind of color chases the breeze of golden leaves.

All of a sudden, it gets quiet and the rain pours down on the fall.

I like to sit by the window in my room and take it all in, you know.

Empty Promises

The days are long and empty. There's no hope in sight.

We tried to work it out, but we can't make it right.

My bed is cold and empty and my heart is torn in two.

What's she got that I don't have? You'll probably use her and dump her, too.

What about all the long promises of how you would be true.

If you call this being true, I sure don't want any part of you.

If I try to find another to take your place. It will be a waste of time, so much of you, I can't erase.

It will take time to heal my broken heart. Then I'm going to take it slow and have a brand new start.

A Disgrace Called War

Tears drop from the cheeks of a little ragged child.

The sounds of guns seem to echo into time as stillness clutches the night.

Darkness surrounds the little one as he lies softly by his Mother's corpse.

He does not understand why his Mother does not respond.

With a timid and fragile hand, he lightly touches her face.

It was cold and unresponding compared to the warmth he had always known.

Grasping her bloody hand, he snuggled up to her breast. His weary eyes close in the silence beneath the stars, the little one sleeps. The war is over but the disgrace will always be remembered by the little one that sleeps.

Little Angels

Where do angels come from?

Do their eyes glitter and shine from the early morning dew?

Are they born under gorgeous rainbows that glow in color for you and me?

Are they rocked to sleep on a morning star so near and yet so very far? They capture rides on the wings of beautiful butterflies while they hum to the sweet sounds of the morning songbird.

Where angels come from I don't know, but I do know it's true.

They sprinkle gold and silver stardust in the hair of beautiful people —- just like you!

Things I Cherish

White wicker baskets full of yellow daisies.
Taking a long nap on a lazy Sunday.
Watching spotted puppies chasing their tail around and around.
Soft music playing my favorite songs.
These are more things I enjoy and cherish.
The smell of a new baby after its nightly bath snuggled under my neck.
To have my house cleaned by a friend when I've been sick and the
house was a wreck.
Soft kisses from the man I love.
Watching the glow of the stars above.
These are all things that make my heart smile.
Life is full of things to enjoy and relax.
Take the time because the years go by much too fast.

Dreams are Real

If time could be saved in a bottle marked with care,
We'd always have an extra day saved to enjoy anytime and anywhere.

Fill a big jar with sunshine and when its supposed to rain, we'll have an extra day to go on a wonderful picnic or soak some sun and fun at the beach.

I'll fill a book full of love and tie it with ribbons of gold. I'll keep it by my bedside in case I found a man I loved.

Dreams are real as life itself and I'll put all my goodies on a shelf. Tomorrow will be beautiful just because I believe in dreams.

In the Present Day

In the eyes of many there is much terror in the city.

Smiles are vacant and eyes look around lost and without hope.

I can't understand if Jesus loves us, why we suffer so much pain and sorrow and it doesn't look any better for tomorrow.

So many storms, hurricanes, and earthquakes. If you think about it, too much you'll go totally insane.

I'll put my faith in Jesus. He'll be coming soon. Anytime they'll be screams of joy because He's come back to take us and make us His angels in the heavens above.

It's Your Choice

Don't fret about tomorrow. Just take it day by day. Life doesn't come easy and God will make a way.

Have faith and believe. He will fill your heart with joy.

Pray that God is with you and soon you will see.

Jesus and His love was meant for you and me. So, believe in our father, his love is true. God's love was made for you.

Tears of joy fill my eyes and my soul is satisfied.

When I live for Christ, He's the joy of my life.

I cherish his holy name and his love is always the same.

Not a burden or a care, He takes all my worries away.

Jesus love me and someday in heaven I'll be with Him

I want to live for Christ. He did the ultimate sacrifice. He paid the price for us to be free.

Living in the Light

Oh, how happy my heart is with thee.
Today I realize the love of God is within me.
He cleansed me of all my sins. A new life now I begin.
I praise His Holy Name. No more do I feel guilt and shame.
I'm living in the light and my soul with God is right.
Oh, how happy my heart is with thee.

Lollipops

I want lollipops but not yellow, purple, or green.

I want a lollipop, the biggest you've ever seen.

I like strawberry, but cherry I love the best. You can just keep all the rest.

I love lollipops that take all day to lick..

The bright cherry flavor will make my tongue thick and my bright lips turn red.

If you don't believe me, watch and see what I said.

I it's my birthday and you don't know what to pick . Give me a dozen cherry lollipops on big sticks.

I don't want a truck or a puzzle or two. A dozen red lollipops will always do. Thank you.

Pearls

I stand on the beach and feel the waves splash against my feet. The beach is a wonderful place for people to meet.

Tides rise and fall and make me feel peaceful inside. I'd love to be able to find a clam on the beach with a pearl inside. A beautiful white pearl, perfect and round. One never knows if they look hard enough, what could be found.

I love to pick up shells of every size and color, but sometimes I step on a sharp rock and boy I can holler.

Even if it cost a hundred dollars, I'd stay at the beach cause it's full of wonder. Peace is found there and I can sit and ponder.

Into the Wind

I've chose to no longer exist.

I've made up my mind to go away —-

Not to a place on this earth, but back to a place I came from first.

No more pain or sorrow , lies, and empty tomorrows.

I chose not to say good-bye, but I'll keep you all close to my heart.

I want my ashes to blow in the wind and be a part of all my God created.

Don't cry a tear that I'm gone. I will go to heaven to be with Mom and Michael.

I thank God for all the people that I've loved and the chance to know so many beautiful people.

As Thyself

Love your neighbor as yourself is a scripture I learned as a child all by myself

I appreciated how kind and lovely some people would teach me.

God knows we keep wishing for more people that can love and see.

Thanks for the joy you brought in our lives.

You'll always be a good memory of joy when I'm down and out.

Wherever you go may He be your guiding light, constant companion, not far from his sight.

Tainted Love

I have to sort through this mess, do what I can and forget the rest.

I know I have to start all over and begin a new life. I'm sure not getting anywhere with your hatred that cuts like a knife.

Sometimes a lot of pain is felt when everything comes to an end, but this has to be all over before you can begin again.

I'll know better not to love and trust them until they've earned that trust.

I'd rather be alone than tolerate this unpredictable pain and suffering.

I know God is with me and I can lean on Him and have faith.

It's going to take a lot of time, but someday I'll be fine and the memories with be erased. Then, they'll be nothing I can't face.

Jader

I have a niece who is so special to me, and when we are talking, I want her to know that she can share anything and be totally free. She's done so many great things to be the person she is.

I love my niece very much and I feel free it will stand the test of time. She shows me she loves me in her own special way.

My home is always welcome in case she needs me.

I'm blessed to have her in my life and she possesses beauty inside and out beyond compare.

I know she loves me and she possesses beauty beyond and compare.

To know I'm a part of her life is great and she can share anything with me and it stays with me, too.

I thank God I've been there as her friend like she's been for me.

No one can come between us and that's the way it will always be.

I may not be her mother, but we have a close bond and she knows I love her like a daughter and I want her to be the best she can be. Someday Jader will be a shinning star for all the world to see.

All my love,
Aunt Leona

After the Rain

Too many major problems, too many days of tears.

I feel overwhelmed and paralyzed by pain, worry, and fear.

I've prayed to God to help me, to give me hope to see.

Someday all this will pass and I'll feel peace again at last.

I have to remember to take one day at a time. Storms don't last forever and once again the sun will shine.

Faith is all I need to lean on and is the most important thing in my life.

Without God I'd be totally lost 'cause He's with me day and night. I just need to let go and give my problems to Him and have faith that I can endure. I know my God loves me and is always there for sure.

Everything in the good book states it always in his time.

So, I'll need more patience to survive the problems and to be able to survive this rat race.

If you take time to help others, it will help you to think less of your pain.

So, hang on and someday soon warm sunshine will come and the dreary days will leave for awhile.

The Dance

Some say weeping willows cry because the wind hurts their branches as it whips the frondi two and fro. I would like to believe for a reason they grow.

To kiss the wind as it tumbles and sways to the beautiful dance of romance. Keeping rhythm to the wind as it sends out a keepsake of vision to taunt and tease the very lovely trees.

Some say weeping willows cry because it hurts their branches. I say it kisses the wind as it tumbles, keeping rhythm to the wind as it tumbles and sways to the beautiful dance of romance.

Let the swift wind carry the branches and I will enjoy their freedom just to be trees.

Colton

Precious little Colton James. Your as beautiful and special as your name. You are adored by friends and family near and far.

I'll bet cha someday you'll be a great sport's star.

Your parents are the best and they'll raise you to love God, sports, and all the rest.

You'll grow up fast because they always do. Someday you'll be a man as the years fly by, too.

You're very loved by all and right now you are small, but watch how fast time will go and someday you'll be a great man.

Tough Times

Everyone has some hurdles and life can be so tough.
It's normal to be down and out when everything is rough.
But there's a silver lining behind every cloud.
So, go ahead and scream and shout, and get your anger out.
Sunshine can't reach dark places and smiles aren't on sad faces.
Just remember this, too, will pass.
God is always with you and His love will always last.

Courage

They say time heals all wounds.
So be patient and stay in tune with your feelings . . . don't run and hide.
Face your fears and they will disappear.
If you feel like crying, then let the tears appear.
We all have feelings of pain and doubt.
I know you know what I am talking about.
Courage is facing your fear, and then, how much better you'll feel.

The Shooting Star

I gazed upon a midnight star and asked my Jesus, "Where you are?"
The star began to sparkle, then it shot across the sky.
It was so magnificent that tears ran down my face.
I cried because I felt God's presence with me. I love this man named.
Jesus, whose Father created the whole human race.
I smiled as I looked to the heavens and wiped the tears on my face.

My Blessing

You give me strength when I am weak.

I can feel your compassion when it's love I seek.

In my prayers, I feel you near by.

When I'm afraid, lonely, and cry,

I asked for understanding and the loneliness fades. Oh, blessings in abundance comes from you above.

I need not worry or fret. You take care of my problems everyday. You're there to help me and show me the way.

Oh, King of Kings, I love you so. How precious you are to me, my love continues to grow.

You are my Savior, and with you by my side, I can do anything and I take it all in stride.

My life is blessed because He lives in my heart. He's my master, and each day, I pray and I have a brand new start.

A Teacher's Prayer

Remember me Lord to be patient. Not all of God's children grow at the same rate.

Strengthen my stride Lord. I put all of myself into this opportunity.

I know they only grow up once. I want to help them, so help me. Make me gentle to their feelings and lighten their spirit.

Teach me to consider both sides.

Bottoms up usually makes the face down. Forgive me when I forget to remember and help me remember to forget.

Bless their differences. Make them proud to be unique.

Inspire them so they learn to love. May they have many blessings from above.

Why Couldn't I See?

You were the one, but I didn't know how the loss of your love would be killing me so.

When I close my eyes, its your face I see. I want you again my love next to me.

I was so blind. Why couldn't I see you had the heart of hearts and was truly meant for me.

Now your gone and I'm so blue. How will I ever make it without you.

I don't think I can make it without your warm embrace. When I held you, I felt safe.

I pray to God that you'll be back and want to love me dear, and that's a fact.

My Heavenly Father

You give me strength when I am weak.
I can feel your compassion when its love I seek.
In my prayers I feel you nearby.
When I'm lonely and afraid, all I do is cry.
I ask for understanding and the loneliness fades.
Oh, blessings come from abundance and I am not afraid.

I need not worry or fret about bills. You always see me through and how much better, then, I feel.

Oh, King of Kings, how fortunate I am to be forgiven for my sins by the blood of the lamb.

Dying Love

The flowers have wilted. Birds no longer sing.

I'm captive of a broken heart and all the pain it brings.

I'll keep on going —- I don't need you anymore.

My heart will never again trust you or love you again.

So many times I'm wondering since I three you out the door, if you go down the line hurting others —- I'm sure of this, I'll find.

So go ahead and hate me when I tried with all my might.

I would give you all I had to give and would have loved you as long as I live.

I gave you so many chances, and everyone you blew.

I don't want anything more to do with you.

Kiss My Softly

Where there's smoke there's fire.
Where there's passion, there's desire.
It only takes a spark to kindle a flame.
I long for your touch. It's driving me insane.
Kiss me softly and hold me tight.
You know how to love me —- so love me tonight.
All day I long for your embrace.
I love you so and long to see you face.
Tonight I'm going to love you like you've never been loved before.
I'll always cherish my girl and still want more.

Angels from Above

Oh, what a glorious place heaven will be.

Angels will be singing choir for you and me.

Heaven is full of love with harps strumming up above.

Waterfalls in pastel colors flow about the land.

Doe and mother deer.

Watch as they stand.

Loved ones holding each other hand in hand.

While they dance and sing to the music from the band.

Oh, what a joy heaven will be to spend the rest of eternity.

I want to go to heaven and be with those I love that already made it to sweet heaven above.

I'll bow down and kiss Jesus' feet and tell Him how happy I am to meet. He will smile and say, My servant, a good Job you have done.

Together we'll walk hand in hand until the evening's done.

Second Fiddle

I don't play second fiddle and its been a week since you walked out the door.

You hurt me so bad. I don't think I want to see you anymore.

I need time to think about what is on my mind.

If I'm supposed to be happy, why am I so blue. I need space to figure out what I'm going to do.

I need and want you, but the other has to go. So make up your mind, but don't take your time.

I may meet someone else who treats me very kind.

Heaven Bound

I dream of heaven in clouds of fluffy white. Angels are singing and everything is right.

I dream of heaven and harps strumming a melody. I just can't tell you how much heaven means to me. We'll see loved one smiling and giving a big hug.

We all dance and sing and, Oh, what a good time we'll have. I want to go to heaven and, Oh what a lovely place it will be.

I hope I see you in heaven and also I hope you'll see me.

No More Tears

I try not to look behind me, and try not to look ahead.

I used to live in the past and many tears I shed.

So, I force a smile upon my face and pray that it will stay.

I'm tired of feeling so lonely and blue.

I know you can feel it, too.

I will try to be happy; not sad or depressed.

I know I can try. I have no reasons why.

I can't go on like this, it makes my friends depressed, too. So I will try to smile, then it will become a habit after awhile.

Mother - Because of You

Because of you I have found a true friend that is there during sunshine and rain.

You make me feel love and feel I belong to a loving family.

Because of you I learned to trust when everyone else did me wrong.

You've been by my side through the sunshine and the rain.

I'll never be able to repay you for what you've done for me. You took me out of the darkness and set my soul free.

Mirror, Mirror

Mirror, Mirror on the wall,
I want to be thinner, younger, and small.
Mirror, Mirror on the wall,
Erase my wrinkles and pull up every thing that falls.
Mirror, Mirror on the wall,
Make my eyes glisten and my nose small.
Mirror, Mirror on the wall,
If you don't hurry up and do it all, your going to go crash from the front room wall.

My Best Friend

God is my best friend, and in Him, I can always depend.

He answers my prayers, but is always just and fair.

My soul hungers and thirsts for the word of God.

My heart is full of love because I have many blessings from above.

He always shows me the right way to go. Oh, I love Him so.

He forgave me of all my sins.

He walks with me again.

God's love will always show me the way,

And with Him, I always want to stay.

Remember Him

I tried to sleep, but problems kept circling in my mind.
I lay awake half the night, and rest, I couldn't find.
Then I remembered Jesus and how much He cares for me.
I got down on my knees and poured my whole heart out to thee.
I cried so hard I couldn't catch my breath.
Then, Jesus spoke and said, "My love one lay down and get some rest.
You need not worry or fret about these many things,
Your faith is abundant and peace it brings."
I got back in my bed without a worry on my mind. I must never forget
About Jesus. In Him, peace I'll find.

My Friend, Momma

Don't tell me not to weep and that it will be alright.
Words like this just anger me and make me want to fight.
When I lot my Mother, all my hope was buried, too.
Now, I feel so lonely and empty. I don't know what to do.
The days are long without her and I'm always feeling blue.
Her laughter and smile would make my day.
Now the Lord has taken her away.
Someday I'll be with my Momma in heaven we'll be. Then, we'll be together for eternity.

Faith

When I am in deep despair and can't find hope anywhere.

I just remember times from the past when I felt the same, and this too, will pass.

I think of my challenges in life and how God gave me strength to endure.

He gave me hope to hold on to cope and gave me more if I needed help.

So remember that the sun is shining bright behind dark and gloomy clouds.

Soon the dark clouds will leave. Just remember to always believe and faith will be your strength to guide you the whole length.

Loving Life

In order for me to live, I have to give.

My heart has known much pain, but in learning to truly love, I have gained.

Sometimes I smile through tears as I think of all the years I've suffered and struggled, but yet kept on going.

Keep love in your heart. Don't let hate tear you apart.

It's easy to be hard and cold, but it'll only make you bitter and old.

So, love all you can. Good people are in demand.

Joy

If I can dream as far as I can dream.
If I have the freedom to be what I want to be.
If I can be happy to have the freedom to dream and to be the best I can be.
Then, true happiness I'll see and joy in life will follow me.

Our Home

Bless this home we love and share.
Where happiness is a part of our normal day.
Our home is the image we reflect.
We're not going to be very happy if its dirty and a wreck.
A home is what you make it and a place to enjoy each day.
Enjoy the blessings of a house filled with love.
It will be blessed from above.

Missing You

I left your coffee cup on the table and it's still filled to the brim.

All around the outside is your red lipstick on the rim.

You said you needed to go, but baby, why didn't you tell me so before you got your diamond ring.

You said, then, that I would always be your king.

Now, I cry all through the night. I thought everything was alright.

So, I'll say a prayer to Jesus to keep you safe and make you see.

You're the only special person in this world made especially for me.

So Special

I hope we'll be together until the end of time. People like you dear are so hard to find.

Honey, you're my whole life. Without you, I couldn't do without.

My heart is yours and your heart is mine. We're very special and one of a kind,

From this day forward you'll always be mine.

Christmas Scrooge

Don't take away the Christmas tree with lights shining bright.

Leave the snowman in a row. The little children made them, don't you know.

I can't believe you don't like Christmas dinner with turkey on a platter or pumpkin pie, it will make you fatter.

Don't stop the Christmas carolers who sing joyfully in the night.

If Santa's sleigh should knock you down, I hope you Scrooge, get out of town.

I can't believe you're such a pity when everyone else feels Christmas giddy.

A Mother's Love

A mother blesses you with her precious love.
Strengthens you with prayers from above.
Encourages you with tender words and care.
Finds time to make you feel special somewhere.
A good mother is a gift your whole life through.
Whatever would we do if we didn't have mothers telling us what to do.

Trust and Believe

We know not what the future holds.

Nor would we be blessed to know whether we will live young or old.

We must live our lives and trust in thee. Things turn out like their meant to be.

God has a purpose for all mankind and we have to trust and believe that he'll give us what we need.

It makes no sense to fret or worry about tomorrow. All it does is wreck our health and fill our life with sorrow.

Just know he loves you and cares and let's keep Him in our prayers.

Reach out and I'll be there to hold your hand. Others may not know but we understand.

I'm not far away. Did I ever leave you long? You always knew I'd be there. I knew where I belonged.

Don't cry for me and miss me. I'm happy in my new life. There's no heartache or sickness. Just reach out and I'll hold your hand. Then when its time to take you, I'll show you this glorious land.

So don't be dismayed. Remember the happy memories. It hurts me to see you cry. I'm not far away and your life here will be over in the blink of an eye. Then I'll be bringing you with me and you'll be happy to go.

Heaven is a paradise and life here is a dream come true.

Moaning Souls

Shadows of their souls hide in dark and murky places.

Moaning out of empty corpses, horror on their faces.

Death calls us all, but who will be the taker. Our father knows the true hearts and leaves behind the fakers. Our time is short and passes by. If he leaves you behind all you can do is cry. So hear my words the day will come when we have to answer to God.

Lets hope you don't get left behind if you knew for sure it would ease your mind.

Devil's Tongue

An angels face and a devil's tongue, now what in the world have I done.
She'll never quit gripping once she's begun.

There's nothing you do that's right and all she wants to do is fight, whether she's wrong or right. I'm so sick of her crappy attitude. I would like to send her down the road.

I can't see how she can even tolerate herself. I think I've had enough and I'll send her on her way.

I can't take her hateful attitude, so no longer will she stay.

Good ridence! And have a nice day.

A Prayer to St. Anthony's Hospital

There's been many millions of prayers said at a hospital that very much cares for the sick ones that fill the halls.

There are so many beautiful hearts that care. You can find them everywhere from surgery all the way to the Housekeeping Dept.

There is lots of love and compassion shown from a hospital that's our very own.

We take pride in the care that's shown. A lot of sickness is cured because God is there when you walk the halls day or night. There's always a smile and a happy face.

God has blessed our hospital and does each and every day because we believe in the goodness and miracles of God. He'll always be there beacon and shining light from a bright, sunny morning through a dark, stormy night.

Inner Peace

Sometimes in the midst of despair you feel like your not getting anywhere. Just find a quiet place inside your mind and learn how to unwind.

Try to let go of all regrets. Calm your thoughts and just reflect. Learn to find inner peace and the turmoil inside will cease.

One of a Kind

I have a daughter who is one of a kind. She's free like the wind and is her own person.

She doesn't follow the rest. She has a heart of gold and ends up doing what she thinks is best.

She has a lot of courage and follows her own path. No one can tell her what to do. She's her own person and doesn't follow the rest.

Her face is like an angel and could light up the darkest day. She is my Angela whose one of a kind. She's my daughter and does what's on her mind.

Stop and Smell the Roses

Take it easy and slow down and rest.

No need to hurry, then you'll be at your best.

Don't wear yourself out in needless worry and despair.

You get farther behind when you're in a hurry to get somewhere.

Life is precious and time can't be replaced. Soon you'll be gone and who will take your place.

A lot of people love you and want you here for goodness sake.

Slow down my special friend and take a little break. Enjoy life that's what God wants you to do. Remember Him —- He loves you, too.

In Times of Prayer

I say many prayers to my Father —- To Him I'm never a bother.

He gives me faith to make it through each day and lifts my burdens in every way.

My Savior always listens when I speak, also when I'm sick and so weak.

He'll heal my illness and make me strong.

He is my redeemer, and to Him, I'll always belong.

All Alone

I'm in a time of despair. I try to find you everywhere.

I'm lonely and I'm blue. Where are you?

You walked out the door and said you weren't coming back. I miss seeing your hat and coat on the rack..

My days are so lonely and long. Here is where you belong. I know you love me, so come back home. Please baby, I don't want to be alone.

Missing Mother

Another winter has come and gone and spring is here again.

This is the season we lost you and it hurts more each year.

I have all the things that should make me happy. But, I lost someone most dear. I no longer have my mother who was like no other.

She was the best friend I had in my life. We loved to talk on the phone. We would talk hours a day and laugh when someone had something funny to say.

Each year that passes I miss her more. We shared lots of laughter and joy.

Silver Lining

Everyone has some hurdles and sometimes life can be so tough.
It's normal to feel down for a while when everything is rough.
But there's a silver lining behind every single cloud.
So go ahead and scream out loud to get the anger out.
Sunshine can't reach dark places and smiles aren't on sad faces.
Just remember this, too, will pass.
And one day you'll realize that sometimes we have to deal with the rain.
Life can be happy, but also full of pain. Turn your rain into sunshine
and change your attitude and to smile and stop being blue.

Faded Love

The reason long forgotten, but the bitterness remains.

Hateful words hastily spoken leaving hearts wounded and broken.

When self-control is lost, our hearts will pay the cost.

Angry looks in a glance. Whatever happened to romance. Pride will keep them from accepting blame. They should both feel shame.

Hate can dowse love from a fire to a flame. They should treat each other with respect and love and ask God to help them be kind and help them from above.

Things I Enjoy

White wicker baskets full of yellow daisies and bows.

Taking a long nap on a Sunday afternoon. Being lazy and watching cartoons.

Watching fluffy puppies chase their tails around the room,

Soft music playing my favorite songs all day long.

These are things I love and cherish and thank God above.

The smell of a new baby after its warm bath.

Happy memories of loved ones in photo albums I don't want to forget.

Soft and tender kisses from the man I love.

Watching the glow of twinkling stars above.

There are many things that make my heart smile.

Life is full of things to enjoy. So take the time to relax for awhile.

The years of our life go by way too fast.

Just take it easy. Slow down and let the good times last.

Times Heals all Wounds

Courage is facing fear even if you're still afraid.

Crying when your sad is alright. Sometimes we all feel uptight.

It's good to laugh every chance you get and enjoy the feelings of laughter before and after.

Time heals all wounds, so have some patience and it will heal the wound.

Time will help get you well. Before long, you'll be feeling swell.

Shooting Star

I gazed upon an evening star and asked my Jesus where you are. The star began to sparkle, then it shot across the sky.

In my heart I felt He said "Where you are, there so am I."

I began to cry and the tears ran down my face. I love this man they call Jesus, whose Father created the whole human race.

Jesus Blessing

With Him I'll always be today, tomorrow and through eternity.

I praise His Holy name and He loves me the same through the sunshine and the rain.

What a blessing to know Jesus is in my heart, no matter what I had to go through, He was beside me,

Oh, I love Him so and want to be in heaven someday.

He always forgives me when I sin. He forgives me and shows me the way again.

Thanks Dad

I am heaven bound and I am fortunate to have learned about God and His love.

I have to thank my father. He had blessings from above.

I will always cherish the way I can lean on God. My Dad is a very special man of God and he worshiped faithfully.

Thank you Dad for showing me the right way.

My respect and love for you I cherish everyday.

My Dad worked hard for all his life. He had to feed children and a wife.

He hung in there both through sunshine and strife.
He'd do what he could to make an extra dollar.

He kept his faith and God was always at his side.

He worked hard on the home and at his jobs and never gave up.

I am so proud of my Dad. He stood for a lot. He talked of Jesus and you could tell he loved Him a lot.

He would have tears in his eyes. He loved him I know. Dad, you deserve a medal for what you have done.

You taught your children responsibility, respect, and told us we were always welcomed home.

Dad made the house home and I'm always glad to come home. We were a big family and Mom loved family.

Please God, let us be together for Thanksgiving and Christmas.

My Little Butterfly

She's a lot like a little butterfly who stops to smell the flowers.

My little butterfly looks over the garden each day and especially likes the roses that are so fragrant.

The rose garden is enjoyed by many people. The garden is her pride and joy and is enjoyed by many people, both young and old.

So thank you littler butterfly for pollinating the flowers. The garden is a good place for prayers.

The sweet flowers grow, and don't you know, they are adored by many people —- especially the beautiful butterflies.

And, the little girl who enjoys the garden everyday.

Dragons

Dragons live among us, so quiet and so still.

Dragons live among us and I know you don't believe me, but it's true.

I can't actually say I have seen them —- for then I would be lying.

I do know that when I want to give up, they kick me right in the rump.

I know they're really there because they always help me through.

They like to curl up and snuggle. Believe me, a dragon really knows how to snuggle.

Yes, they snore loud but it's their breath that will kill you every time.

So you have to be a fighter to sleep with a dragon.

And anyway, dragons love us more than anyone could. I only need one dragon and she does the job quite well.

Here lately, he's been very busy kicking me in the rump.

But, if you too get down in the dumps, you can borrow my dragon for awhile.

He comes very highly recommended to people in the dumps who need kicked in the rump.

Sunflowers

If we were flowers in a garden by the pond, I'd hope that you were planted next to me.

We'd be together like sunflowers smiling all summer long.

With our faces turned to the sun and the birds will sing a beautiful song.

Heaven Knows

In every ones life there is someone who is thought of as Dear.

Days are long and nights are lonely if you are not near.

Heaven knows I love a someone who also cares for me.

Nothing can be changed or rearranged the feelings are pure and real.

I'll wait a lifetime and He knows how I feel.

I am good for him and he's good for me, so we should be together heaven knows.

All I have to do is look at his face. When we're together it's almost like it glows.

We need each other like a rose needs water. I will love him forever, heaven knows.

Jesus

There came a man from Bethlehem who had love for all mankind.

He was a very simple man, you understand, but yet over time he changed the world.

Jesus is His name and He's still the same and even will be today and tomorrow.

He talked of love and kindness and healed many people of blindness. He even made the crippled walk.

Yes, Jesus did many miracles, yet He was the best miracle of all. Jesus spoke softly, yet the things he said have made it around the world.

I love my precious Jesus because He saved me from the grave. He lifts me up when I'm feeling low and always guides me on the right way to go.

Do you know Jesus, too. He knows you through and through.

If you reach out a hand, I know he'll understand.

He forgives without hesitation and accepts you just as you are.

He'll always love you and will never forsake you. What He promises is all true.

Give your hand to the Man from Bethlehem.

However you are, he understands. With Jesus, there is no greater love.

Let Jesus into Your Heart

Too few, too far, more pain, another scar.

Life hurts and spits us out.

I'm sure you know what I'm talking about.

Keep on trying to take in stride. The reasons why I can not hide.

Too few, too far, more pain, another scar.

Things seem hazy and out of focus.

It doesn't help to say hocus-pocus.

Rivers run deep in the midst of despair.

Especially when it looks like you're not getting anywhere. Too few, too far, more pain, another scar.

Give your heart to our Father and start out right.

He loves you with all his might and will stand against the devil. For your soul he'll fight.

God loves you so much, why don't you just hold out your arms. Let the Holy Spirit embrace you and keep you from all harm.

Jesus died on the cross so you can be forgiven from all your sins.

He is the greatest of all men. Let Jesus show you the right path to follow.

He is the truth and the light. He cared for you and wants you to give up the drugs and alcohol and fight.

Heaven waits for you and there is a place saved just for you.

Reach out your hand and Jesus will heal you. He is so Devine. Won't you come to Jesus now.

He waits for you and is knocking at your door.

Tell the devil to hit the road. Your soul belongs to Jesus now.

You have the power to change your life.

He'll be with you through sunshine and strife.

Won't you take Jesus' hand? He'll turn you into a brand new man.

Take his hand. Jesus will forgive you because He understands.

Let your light shine bright and love the good Lord with all your might..

The Question of Life

God, is life meant to be hard? Is trouble the dragon to slay?

Does each sunrise bring more pain or more grief? The days are long and weary Lord.

My heart longs for peace and tranquility. My soul yearns to be free.

Is time a scale on which eternity never ends?

Or, is life a scale on which time weighs?

Is beauty and love an illusion of man's strings afar for escape?

Can a minute be stalled Lord, so I can catch my breath?

Life is a strong wind at my breasts. I gasp to breath, but still it labors.

The path of life is harder to follow.

Time is running near. I need some strength to fight my way among the good paths above.

The winds of time are furiously blowing. I seem to have lost my way; or is this the time for me to be called home.

A Place in Heaven

Tears shared with laughter.

A life ever after.

Just waiting for my time

A place in heaven will be mine.

My Lord is always with me and in Him I can confide.

Through prayer I can reach Him when I feel companionship and know He is there.

Jesus blesses and heals the sick, weary, and blind.

I love my Lord Jesus. He is my refuge when times are hard.

He's my redeemer because he forgives me of all my sins.

There is nothing or nobody I can trust in this old world except God.

There is nothing I like more than God, the angels and my precious heaven above.

My Savior

He is the everlasting Savior of my life and of my soul.

I lean on Jesus when problems make their toil.

I cherish my heavenly Father through the bad times and the good.

Prayer lifts me when I'm sick, worried, or sad.

He'll fill your head and heart with peace if you just make amends.

Take the time to worship Jesus and He'll take the *time* for you.

Someday you'll be very sick and you'll call out His name.

If you're a friend of Jesus, He'll put sunshine in your life and take away the rain.

On this earth He's my strength and master and I'll be with him forever after.

Color

Color a gorgeous rainbow that stretches across blue skies.

Add color to white butterflies and make them bigger and brighter than it's size.

Make zebras polka dots instead of stripes of black and white.

Paint a green meadow purple with colors of daisies as you lay in the soft grass on your back.

Bright orange roses would be quite a change from their regular pink, white, yellow, or red.

Pretend and make it happen. You'll see how color changes, how we feel. Try it and you'll see that it's real.

Deep Scars

Sometimes I try to be so hard.

Not wanting to care much because I don't want to hurt anymore.

But slowly I break.

My green eyes fill with tiny pebbles and slide down my face and pile around my feet on the floor.

Just when I had reached stone cold apathy,

My frozen heart thaws to expose some very deep scars. I care not to ever care if it means another broken heart.

No Heart

There are quiet places in hearts and faces, which no longer feels.

There become puddles of tears from all the years of hurt and sorrow. No hope lives even for tomorrow. It will all be the same; nothing will change except to drive me totally insane.

No thanks, I've had enough and I'm so drained.

Eyes that search. Hands that reach out. We've learned to let go and to see what really is and I know will always be.

Total vanity is his crime. In later years, his looks will fade.

No one will be around because he as no heart. No one will be around this is true. He has no heart except for himself. Now everyone knows the truth.

Fool Out of Me

The days are long and empty. There's no hope in sight.

My bed is big and cold and my heart is torn into. You were my whole world, then you left and made me blue —- I'm so mad at you.

Now, not a thing I care to do.

I tried to start another relationship. They can't take your place.

Someone else can't make me happy and I have so many memories I can't erase.

The love we shared was precious, or have you forgot already?

The special times we shared and the diamond ring you brought me. You said you love me and I feel like I'm dying slowly.

Couldn't we try just one more time to work it out? We're good for each other and you know what I'm talking about.

I don't feel like there is any hope in sight.

We're good for each other and you know what I am talking about. I never thought for a minute things would work out this way.

I think I'll get all dressed up and go out for dinner. I'm tired of living in despair. I have to get on with my life.

It won't be the same without you, but life goes on whether we like it or not.

Today

Today, I feel like I don't want to feel. But then, staying in bed all day is a good choice because of how I feel.

A cup of coffee sounds good right now.

If only it would come walking down the hall with a little cream and sugar tagging behind.

If I slide both feet on the floor, I could follow them out the door.

Oh well . . . this place called the bedroom is my, for today, temporary sanctuary.

Have you ever wondered before why they don't call it a rest room instead.

The window shades hide the afternoon sun and the evening sun, too, for all I care.

Today I don't want to feel. I'm just going to roll over and pull blankets over my bead.

What? I don't care?

No, I think it's just the opposite. I've cared too much.

Now, I'm going to care for me.

Good night or good day, whatever you want to call it.

A Dark Stranger

I saw you from a distance surrounded by a black cloud, and as I came closer, you screamed out loud.

Your trembling voice was so filled with sorrow, that it made me cry.

You just needed understanding. I had plenty to borrow.

When I held you, I could sense your pain and I understand what your darkness was all about.

Tears just flooded from your eyes and you cried on my shoulder. You held me so close I thought I would break.

I had plenty of love, compassion, and understanding. You had a lot to talk about to empty the darkness you felt.

Together, we fell asleep on the couch and I think he was doing better and felt safe.

As the days went by and a season passed; he felt better and we fell in love. Soon you smiled a lot and the darkness faded.

I am glad that I took the time to help him. Now, we go everywhere together and he's very grateful for my concern. I'm glad I helped him and he has become the center of my world.

No Fool

As the tears fell softly from my eyes. I just couldn't say good-bye.

It was even hard to speak, because my pain had reached an all time high.

Just go on ahead and walk away. I knew you'd steal my heart, and then someday, go away.

Don't look back as you walk out the door . . . cause my heart can't take anymore.

I feel like a fool that's been used. You'd think I'd get use to being used. Someday, you'll cry and want me back.

I won't be a fool and let you drain me dry. How you could be so cold and act as if you don't care? I guess you never loved me and lied. All I have to say is good-by.

Just Another Day

Time seems to be suspended in air; weight-less and empty, only visible to the sad and lonely to beckon its passing.

Hours reluctantly drain into passages that show light and then darkness.

A day does not seem like a beginning or an ending, but only small segments they call time that cast shadows on my tears at night and the darkness seeps into chasms of despair.

Again, it's another day. Just another day.

Dreams

Follow your dreams; all it takes is a start. Before too long you'll hear a song in your heart.

Dance to the music along the way. If you follow your dreams, your song will stay.

Heart Me Now

Hear me now before the night rides in and gathers together the empty shadows.

Faded together in hews of desperate grays; they slide slowly down; these painted walls.

They linger and taint me until dawn.

The walls grow smaller. The walls grow colder. They sigh as they hold in all my pain.

Hear me now, for tomorrow maybe too late. The thought won't stop.

As I cry out into the darkness, I feel they may consume me before the night rides in.

Hear me now, please, hear me now.

Walls that grow smaller.

Walls that grow older as the pain becomes stronger; the night becomes longer, until one day morning may never come.

Here me now, please hear me now, before it's too late.

Have Faith

There is no greater love than the love given from our Savior above.

No matter what day or hour He is the power and shows how much He cares. He will always listen to our prayer.

When I am weary, hopeless and blue, I remember to pray to Jesus and He makes me feel new.

Jesus gives me peace and makes me feel whole. I dedicated my life to him. He is the master of my soul.

Take the time to talk to Jesus. He knows how you feel. I love my precious Jesus. I have faith in Him and know He is real.

Isaiah - a Dream Come True

They are a good family who are Christians and couldn't have children of their own.

They became foster parents, but it hurt to love a child , then have to give them up.

They took in Isaiah and I don't mean maybe; he became the child of their dreams and they loved him like a son.

As he became older they felt like they were all a little family.

Then came little Ava who needed lots of care.

Then they had a boy and girl and really felt like a family.

Lori and Clayton became the best parents you can find anywhere.

For years they had to fight Isaiah's Dad in a custody battle.

They hung together and wouldn't give up the battle to get Isaiah.

They showed strength and faith and would not buckle in. Their love for Isaiah made them fight to the end.

I look up to this sweet family for the love they gave and the sacrifice they made.

Isaiah is lucky to have such a wonderful Mom and Dad.

They became a beautiful little family, who with God's help, made their dreams come true.

Tell My Heart Lies

If you want to leave me, please softly let me go. Take the time to be kind. My heart has been broken many times.

I keep thinking of you. I keep thinking of you and the good times we had. I have to let you go. Broken hearts don't mend well.

It seemed we were in love and had God's blessing. I know God cared. I often talked to Him in prayer.

I feel so empty and full of pain. If I don't get any rest, I feel like I may go insane.

If you never loved me; why did you tell me so. It will take a long time to be happy again, you know.

So good-bye, take care. I promise I'll tell my heart and tell it I don't care, but it will always show.

Peace in Heaven

Please take me home to a mountain stream so fresh and pure. Let me lay down in soft green grass and my problems will vanish for sure.

Fill my soul with peace divine. Forever more heaven waits and the angels are so very kind.

No more suffering will I have. I'll soon be taken into God's hands.

God has no boundaries for the love he shares. He will be there forever because He cares. God is always there.

The Bible speaks of the love and peace He gives if you come unto Him.

I have a gift to look forward to when Jesus calls me home. I'm ready to finally know heaven and to be free from pain.

Follow Jesus

The day that Jesus died the sky was black as He hung crucified. But still, they were not satisfied.

Jesus spent his whole lifetime sharing what God wanted Him to say.

But still, people won't listen. They have to do it their own way.

I want to follow Jesus and share the cross He carried. It's lighter than eternity in hell.

God blesses my life everyday. With Him I always want to stay and will be well.

Butterflies

(Dedicated to Mom —- she loved Butterflies)

Butterflies always fill me with delight. So carefree as they go up and take flight.

They dance around the beautiful flowers and spread their wings in the soft breeze that blows, never sad, always happy and it shows.

I can't believe they start out as an ugly caterpillars and crawl from their cocoon after a short period of time. He crawls from his cocoon and, like magic, they fly into the sky with radiant color. Then they play without care.

You can't find them when you want to. They are here and zip, they're gone. They are part of the summer landscape just as the songbird sings so sweetly. Beauty is a gift from God. Enjoy it!

Chuck-a-Luck

I have a brother like no other. He's got a heart of gold. He is always doing favors for people and won't take anything in return.

He's found Jesus and his life has turned around. Drinking too much causes problems. This now, he understands.

I call him everyday and I'm always glad to hear him laugh and to hear what he has to say.

His luck has turned from bad to good. Chuck is always polite and treats people like he would want to be treated.

He's learning to leave the past behind him and he's a lot more cheerful. I only wish him the best and hope he gets his license and car and job.

I hope God looks over Chuck and keeps him to get back on the track. I pray for his complete and lasting recovery.

He's a new man and is trying the best that he can. I'm proud of Chuck for changing his life. It took a lot of fortitude, but he did it with God's help.

I love my brother and he's a special friend. I'm blessed to have him in my life. He needs to ask God for strength and will power. Nothing is impossible with God.

The Winter of My Life

This is truly the winter of my life. The chill of reality slithers down my spine. Cold and empty faces stare into the space that divides my soul from theirs.

My existence with the ones with stone cold eyes has left me restless and afraid.

I fear they shall consume my heart and deny me the right to feel.

This passage they call life does not heed my cries. I lost my dreams in the bitter blatant past; but it carries me on.

I stumble into the blowing frozen night and wonder through my past.

My footprints begin to blow away and I become part of the cold midnight air.

My Dad

I have a father like no other. He helps my three sisters and five brothers whenever he can.

He is always there with a kind smile and he believes in Jesus very strongly.

He gives advice and lends a helping hand. He has integrity, knowledge and faith.

I have many good memories of the things he has done to help me.

He'll always be a trooper and has always stood his ground.

He liked to have fun and laugh, especially when all the kids are together. He is full of joy.

He's healthy and has lived a very long life. Someday he'll be buried by his much-loved wife.

Someday I'll see them again in heaven. We'll all be a family again if we all live right. Dad will worship Jesus until God calls him home. We'll miss him terribly, but he will be in a much better place.

Relax

Hush the flood of noises you hear and learn to relax and give your worries to God.

Don't hold onto the memories that cause you pain when a bad thought protrudes, then try to refrain.

Take care of your mental pictures that cloud good thoughts in you mind.

If you do these things and practice to mentally relax; the rest of the body will do the same.

Remember to pray and ask for strength and peace and soon the negative thoughts will cease.

A Prayer from Mom

Reach out and I'll be there to hold your hand. Others may not know, but we understand.

I'm not far away. Did I ever leave you long? You always knew I'd be there where I belong.

Don't cry for me and miss me. I'm happy here in heaven. There's no sickness or sorrow, no fear of tomorrow.

Reach out and I'll be there to hold your hand. Then, when its time to take you, I'll show you this beautiful land.

So do not be dismayed. Remember the happy memories. It hurts me to see you cry. I'm not far away and your life here will be over in a blink of an eye.

The Loss

I understand your sorrow, grief and pain. Whenever you lose a loved one, nothing is the same.

Loss leaves one full of emptiness and despair. My prayers are with you that God finds you comfort in these days of despair.

To Dad

Here are nine smiling faces and time never erases the knowledge and wisdom that we learned from you. As we grew older, we became aware you taught us to care, to love, and to share.

Now that we are married and have children of our own, we can handle responsibility because of what you had shown.

So, we want to teach our children the virtues we have learned from you.

When we thank the Lord for all our blessings, you're always included in there, too.

My Best Friend

Let's enjoy what time we have left on this earth and I can positively make a bet that we'll all be in heaven someday soon.

So, remember always you're my best friend and I will love you until the end.

Thanks for everything you've done for me. I can never make it up to you.

I couldn't start to do what you have done to make myself feel good about being one.

So, I wish you all the best of luck because you deserve the finest.

There's just something about you that makes you different from the rest.

It's probably your big heart. I could tell you had one from the start.

So, here's to life and love and the moon and the stars above. Especially to heavens where we'll dwell. They'll be no pain or suffering of any kind.

Take good care of yourself and I'll do the same for me. Best friend, you're one of a kind and you are always on my mind.

A Man Very Loved

Jesus was a poor man who walked from town to town. All He had was love and wisdom and soon word got around.

Jesus loved all people; whether leprosy, cripple or blind. He was a loving and kind man. The best you'll ever find.

He healed many people and did God's wishes without hesitation.

He's the King of Kings and the inspiration of many nations.

Jesus was without sin. He died on the cross to set us free from sin.

Won't you let Jesus in your heart? He died for you and me.

Your salvation is the greatest gift. Accept Jesus and the gift is your, too. That's all you have to do.

Echoes

Down below I hear an echo of days long gone by. Children's voices involved in play bounce from the brick walls.

The sounds of the children's laughter drift off. Just like my childhood thoughts escaped into the back of my mind.

Sometimes peeking out to remind me that it doesn't hurt to have fun like a child again. At least for just one day.

Oh, if only to be able to run in the meadows, like I did as a child.

Barefoot and carefree, not yet scarred by the pain I would somehow endure between then and now.

To be able to chase the biggest monarch butterfly and giggle as it teased playfully in the breeze.

The Spirit of a Child

A child sees the beauty in all and accepts those things they know to be true.

It is painful to recall the past that made me forget the child in me now.

To be happy, one must remember to bless the small miracles. One sees so many as a child.

Through knowledge and experience, one begins to grow and change.

One learns to analyze and calculate life. One forgets, unlike the child to believe in life and trust.

Maybe it is too much adversity that changes the child in us all.

As a child, life is full of fire. Days seem endless and so does the wonder in their eyes. Their candle is full of light. Time and adversity wait to beckon its flames to the wind.

When one learns that life is not always there of calmness and beauty; the winds of time can now capture the flame of the spirit.

It will be the strength of belief and hope that keeps the flame burning through life.

Illusions

We try to think that eventually things will work out fine.

But, their only illusions in your mind in this life, we are meant to struggle and then we'll look forward to heaven.

We try to trust others, but they only tell you what you want to hear.

Just always know that Jesus is always near and is the only one you can truly trust.

To try to find joy here is just an illusion and its best to put your treasures in heaven where they belong.

Someday you will die, and then, realize that you are glad you learned. This world is a temporary place and a big rat race.

Believe in Jesus. He is real and he will welcome you with open arms. Then, finally you will be free from harm.

True Love

I know you cared so much for me and your love was real.

Someday you'll be in heaven, so wait for me and then we will embrace and shout with much joy.

In heaven you don't have to suffer anymore.

Loving You

Love has found its way into my heart.
When our eyes met, I loved you from the very start.
Now, I have a love in my life.
We'll share the good times and the bad.
I found joy when I met you.
And I know you feel this way, too.

The Light

Go towards the light and keep up the good fight.
When you stumble in the night,
Get yourself up —- you'll be alright.
If you're in pain, you'll wonder if the time is right.
When you wake up, go towards the light,
And remember things are either wrong or right.
Go towards the light and believe in Him with all your might.
Whether it be day or night, always go towards the light.

Finding Jesus

We must pray to our Father for the bread we eat.
We must pray to our Father for a restful sleep.
Our Father hears our prayers when we are sick, tired or blue.
He shall always love us just as we love Him, too.

Where Are You?

In time of despair I try to find you everywhere.

I'm lonely, scared, and blue. Where are you?

You walked out the door and said you weren't coming back.

I just thought you were mad and would really take me back.

Where are you now that my heart is broke in two?

It's been three long days and I haven't heard a word.

I need you now more than you know.

When we made love I thought my love showed.

Where are you now? I've cried until I'm sick.

Of all the mean things you could do . . . making me worried so bad has left me lonely, blue, and mad.

I thought you loved me, too, or is this your way of saying good-by. You owed me more respect than that. You're nothing but a dirty old rat.

Catch Me

Will you catch me when I fall? Is there anyone I can depend on at all?

I need to know, so please don't answer so slow.

I need someone who cares.

Is there any one out there?

I'm lonely and so blue. I need someone who is true.

Would you catch me when I fall? Will you be there when I call?

I'm not wasting any more time with you. You show no concern or respect.

So stay away. I don't want you back. You're a cheating two-time loser.

That's all I have to do is tell you to stay away. You don't deserve to be treated so cold. His games are getting old.

Trust and Believe

We know not what the future holds. Nor would we be blessed to know.

We just must trust. What will be, will be and let the boat row. We must live our lives and trust in Thee.

God has a purpose and time for all mankind and we have to trust and believe.

What he'll give us is what we need. Makes no sense to worry or fret about tomorrow. All it does is wreck our health and fill our lives with sorrow.

Trust your faith. Life is both good and bad. No sense in being mad or sad. Just know that He loves you, and in this, always be glad.

Help My Say Good-bye

A place in my heart you made from the very start.

You were sweet and funny and we didn't have any money.

God know's you can't buy love.

I found time went so fast as the years passed. We still didn't have much money, but somehow we would last.

Many, many hours we'd sit and talk and share a laugh or two. I felt safe with you. You became ill and I stayed by your side. I did what I could to help you get by. I had my hands full, I won't lie.

My health got worse, but still I stayed by your side through thick and thin. We'd battle it out, and then, make amends.

Now they took you to a home and I'm lost and all alone. We had many years together and now we're torn apart.

Can you help me please to say good-by?

My heart will always belong to you, my love; until the day I die.

Can you help me to say good-by?

The Angels Dance

Late at night on the old porch swing in the stillness of the night, Michael would play is guitar and sing.

The stars and the moon knew *well* many times.

As Michael relaxed on the old porch swing, the crickets sang right along with him.

Michael didn't want for much. Just peace inside his head. He suffered most from his disease. When Michael laid down to get some sleep, the voices stole his world as he laid in bed and curled around the blankets and told the voices to let him be. He can't get his rest being up all night. So, he'd wait for dawn to come, then the voices would subside some.

We can't even imagine the torment he went through day and night.

Michael wanted to be a star and look down on us as he sings his lullabies.

Michael was a kind and sweet son and in heaven is where he belonged.

Now angels dance to Michael's songs. He tells them of us all and waits for us while the angels dance to his favorite songs.

Missing You

Autumn leaves dance as I think of our romance.

Swirling in a circle, the leaves act happy as I leave the park to go.

I'll be glad when you're gone. I miss you terribly.

I'm so lonely and blue that I don't know what to do.

I miss your smiling face. It's engraved in my mind. Nothing can take its place.

Your hugs and kisses made me fill very loved. I know we had blessings from our Father above. When I see you I'll run into your arms. I love you so much. I feel safe with you and free from harm.

The Gift

I met an ole man down on a dusty country road.
He held out his hand and told me to do exactly what I was told.
I looked in my hand and there laid a gold ring.
He said if I used it right great riches it would bring.
I thanked him for the gift and he waved as he turned the bend.
I couldn't figure all this out, but understanding would come in time.
I wonder mostly why I met this old man whom I would eventually call him a friend.

The ring was meant to remind me to think of others before they fall.
I inherited a large estate and gave it to a dozen homeless people.
I had build a beautiful little country church with a big white steeple
The ore I gave the more I got. It seems like the riches never stop.
I still wear the ring and I have a very loving and big heart.
The ring is a constant reminder that any gift is beautiful if it is given in love and beauty and these are never apart.

The Angel

I met a man from Galilee who stared into my eyes like he was looking right through me.

He asked if I knew of my redeemer, pure of spirit and never a sinner. He was blunt and wasted no time. He laid his questions on the line.

Who was this man and what did he want from me?

He asked me about my salvation and was I baptized to wash away my sins.

I said, yes I do know Jesus and I know that he loves me. I told him I believed in salvation and was baptized as a child.

The man smiled and shook my hand. He told me to share what I know about Jesus to people across the land. I became a minister and people came from miles around to hear me talk about Jesus and salvation.

Who was this man I met who inspired me to preach?

I'll never know for sure, but I think it was an angel of God who was sent to make a big change in me.

We are What We Think

If a man is what he thinketh, then I'll have to watch my thoughts.

My head is always pounding and my tummy's full of knots. If I try to give the day my best and it doesn't go my way, I'll force a smile upon my face and hope that it will stay.

It takes practice to be happy, but it will all be worthwhile when my car breaks down in the middle of town and I just sit and smile.

Freedom

I was like a butterfly trapped in a cage. I knew my Mom felt like me at an early age.

She loved butterflies and, like the butterfly, wanted to be set free.

I was like Momma and wished I could be.

Like everyone else to a certain degree. Momma said it's OK to be different like me.

To be yourself is a gift you see.

So, I loved Momma, and best of all, learned to love me.

Michael

If I could go back in time for just a few hours, I'd spend this special time with you.

We'd sit and write songs for you to play on your guitar. If you hadn't had your disease, you would have become a star.

But that doesn't matter to me because you're the biggest star in the galaxy to me.

I know you're in heaven and traded your white cowboy hat for a crown. Someday soon I'll see you around.

You suffered so and now you're able to be whatever you want to be.

I'll always cherish you, my son. Wait for me and we'll be together again. I love you.

They'll Never Be Another You

I never noticed how much you sacrificed to make our house a home.

It meant so much just to add a little touch while you spent your time alone.

The world kept going as you watched by the windowsill.

You were content in the little world you created.

You couldn't be gone long because you worried about your pet dogs and getting back home.

When we gathered together, you were always full of laughter. You said nothing means more than family.

I cherished the memory of your smiling face and how you liked to joke. Time will never erase.

I feel such a loss without you here because of the cherished memories in our hearts and so dear.

Thank you Mom for just being you. There'll never be another you.

Friend

I've got a friend with a heart of gold and we'll be telling jokes until we grow old. It amazes me how much we're alike . . . because we're always doing things the same. We both get down when it rains. We both like to cook and clean house. We both like pets and kids and it's hard for both of us to be thin. I'm glad you're my friend. I'll cherish you until the very end.

My Dear Mother

She was a woman who loved to laugh. She was a woman who cried a lot about her past.

She had a mother who died giving her life. She had a father who rejected her and it cut like a knife.

She always wanted a family and a home. God blessed her with many —- she was never alone.

Five boys and four girls became her family. She worked all the time to take care of the home.

Dad always worked many jobs to bring money home. It was tough to feed nine kids, but we did it as much as we could alone.

Although we didn't know it then, we learned a lot from them. We thanked them for the hard work and worry they endured. We had it tough, but God saw us through. I appreciate what my parents did when I was just a kid.

Heroes

Where are the heroes that used to stand tall. I look back and I them all. We respected and honored their name, as they played their part in life's game.

Where are all the heroes that use to stand tall. They became a legend and then they would fall.

We need to have some heroes that we can call our own. To make a mark in our lives and even in our homes.

Will someone be our hero so we can all stand tall and proud.

I'm an American and am used to heroes in my life. So, lets find some heroes at least four or five.

The River

Love is like a river that flows deep within your soul. If you don't cherish it, the river will turn cold.

Sometimes adversity makes us cry and there are many reasons why.

You should lean on Jesus when all you can do is sigh.

Giving love to others will turn the river warm.

Never blame Jesus for your problems I for warn.

He'll help you in your distress and sometimes carry you until there's sunshine on the river and you're no longer blue.

I Like It When It Rains

Dark clouds gather over the pond up the road. I can hear the crickets and a trio of big green toads.

Tops of trees are swaying and dancing in the breeze.

There's a whirlwind of color as the winds chase the breeze and leaves.

The sky finally cries as big raindrops fall.

I like all the seasons, but best or all, I like fall.

Michael David

Time goes by as I cry for my Michael David. He went to Jesus and you've got to believe us. He's in a better place now.

My heart misses him so. I often feel like I don't know if I can make it without him.

Someday in heaven I'll run in his arms. Until then, Jesus keep me from harm.

I have to thank God that I had him thirty-one years, as I wipe away the tears.

I was so proud of him. He was the joy of my life. He was by my side through both joy and strife.

So Michael, I say, "See ya later" until Jesus calls me home. Then my life will be full of love when I am taken up above.

Jesus in My Life

In my shadow He guides my day. He's there to put me on the right road when I stray.

I am never alone if Jesus is in my life. I'm trying to do what's right.

Other people mock and laugh, but they don't understand. His glory and all. He does on my behalf.

I have faith in Jesus and He lifts me above my troubled time. Jesus is my life and means the whole world to me.

My Father

I love my Father. He's a great man. He taught me how to live and that's why I am loving, giving, and care for others.

He worked hard to please my Mother. She died five years ago and he'll have now other.

He cherishes Jesus and has him in his heart. He has a place in heaven with Mother. Together they'll be in glory land forever.

Thank you Father for what you've done for me.

I'll be your daughter and friend for all eternity.

Remembering Him

When your wishing on a shining star, always keep our God in your plans. He'll take you farther than any star.

Far and near, He's the best. I'll promise you now, forget about all the rest.

Loving Him will warm your soul especially when adversity in life takes its toll.

Keep in mind He's always at your side. It's his earth, we're just here for the ride.

You'll ride to heaven if you do God's will.

Just believe and be silent and listen to the still.

My Special Friend

When I have dark and empty days and my future seems but just a haze. I have a friend who knows just what to say, or not to say at all.

Sometimes when I've had it over my head with problems I cant seem to shed, my friend is right there sharing life's burdens with me.

She can always make me laugh when I'd thought I'd forgotten to. Through the years, sharing both laughter and tears; my heart holds this friend very dear.

She always believed in me, even when I stopped believing in myself.

God has blessed my life in many special ways. Having a best friend who is also my sister is very special to me.

Cheers

Hand me a cold beer or a glass of sweet grape wine. Give me a couple re-fills and I'll be feeling fine.

They can keep their champagne and martini with a twist of lime.

I like to live simple and that goes for my brew, too. I don't need no cocktail parties with long stemmed glasses.

I'll take my cans right out of the cooler and pop open a can. It's the best in the land.

One Chance

We don't hold destiny in our hands. It slips through your fingers like grains of sand.

Take heart and remember we've only one chance at life. Don't take it for granted cause we're her for just a while.

Take heed the Master may call you home, but just remember, you're never alone.

The Big Change

Not too long ago I was sad and blue and didn't know what I should do.

For years I felt so empty and afraid. My life seemed life seemed hopeless and I laid in bed all day.

I had no energy. I was lifeless and afraid. I had to make the first move to straighten up my mess. I guess I was slowly deteriorating in the state I was in.

So, I decided to get cleaned up and go to a new church where I have never been before.

I prayed hard and cried and asked God to help me.

I turned my whole life over to Jesus and H gave me a brand new start.

Now that I have Jesus, my life has turned around. I have a job, a family, and I still remember when I was so lonely and destitute, I didn't know where to begin. I have a new start now and I feel wonderful.

Close Friends

I want close friends who will make me laugh when I'm down.

Who's by my side through thick and thin and they are hard to find.

I've had a few good friends in my lifetime and they're the best thing I can find.

Sometimes you're so close you can read each other's mind.

To have good friends you have to be one and money just can't buy the closeness of a true friend and all the emotional ties.

I have a good friend named Linda, who is also my big sister. I love her and respect her and she feels the same way I do.

A Special Place

I know there's a special place that someday I'll go.

It's beautiful and full of love.

When I'll go, I don know.

Life here is hard and I cry all the time because I'm alone. Then, I tell myself Jesus is with me whenever I roam.

I ask Jesus for guidance and pray for forgiveness when I need to.

He's there to lighten my load when I'm tired, sick, and blue.

If you had a friend like Jesus you'd understand the love.

He's always there with you sending love from above.

Time to Mend

It takes time for people to grow. It takes time for people to mend. You get through a major crisis, then it starts all over again.

We get stronger and endure life's pain longer.

When we grow older, we become a soldier and keep our weapons close at hand.

It takes time for people to grow. It takes time for people to mend.

Keep the faith and persevere. God will be with you to the end.

My Blessing

In everyone's life there is someone who God blesses to share love.

Knowing my need for someone strong, persistent and full of love, He gave me you.

Yesterday, you gave me strength to live.

Today you give me persistence to cope.

God has given many things that have blessed my life, but best of all, He gave me you.

Tic Toc

Seasons change and our lives are rearranged.

Summers come to pass, then snow builds up fast.

We continue to strive even when all hope has passed us by.

We cry tears we don't feel and smiles that aren't real, and we still survive.

When all we feel is pain, what is there to gain.

Listening to the clock go tic toc, tic toc.

We sleep into noon and get in a day of gloom, and still the clock tics.

Love Everlasting

The scriptures tell the story of the glory of the Lord.
How He performed His many miracles and lived to share the love that
God has so deeply for us.

Won't you be a part of God's loving family and join in everlasting faith
and peace.

Then, you will also share the story of His glory and testify for thee

How Can I Say Good-bye?

If I went away, would I be able to leave the pain or would it follow me along and slowly drive me insane. I never thought it would be so hard to say good-by to you.

But, all I do is pace the floors and wonder what to do.

We can't live together and we can't live apart.

There seems to be no answer, but to begin a brand new start,

I hope someday that I'll look back and time will heal the pain.

I walk out the door and feel the cold blowing rain on my face.

I see you at the window and I slowly drive away. I feel my heart will break, but you know I can't stay.

Someday we'll both find someone new, but I know I'll never stop missing you.

We can't live together and we can't live apart.

There seems to be no answer, but to begin a brand new start.

Went Away

Somewhere in the distance I lost myself.

Yesterdays, todays, and tomorrows all had to do with just time.

The emptiness I felt was the only feeling I could feel. So, I went away alone.

Not to hide, but to find that feeling that belongs to people that know inner peace. It cannot be given to you by the best of friends or purchased by the richest person you could find.

It came to me by just being me, when I went away alone.

My Michael

My child, my son, I will always cherish the memories. When I close my eyes, I remember. There is sunshine in your smile that warms my heart.

Michael, my son, I will never forget the good times we had together.

Remember the huge snowman we built together on turkey day of '81? Yeah! That was a masterpiece of solid snowflakes. It was 6 feet tall and we used black charcoal briquettes for his eyes.

What the heck, we had fun and got a big laugh from it anyway. I even had a real cigar in its mouth with a crooked gangster look on his face.

We used a matching blue hat and scarf. The hat blew off after a hard struggle to tug it on its head. We kept it off after that.

Do you remember how cold our fingers and toes were when we finished?

We were so proud of our huge snowman. You stood in front of the white sculpture while I took the picture. I could have sworn he winked at me before I got the shot. Yep! Those were to good ole days.

Angela

Angela, Angela, where are you going now? What is it you are looking for? Can we help you somehow?

Getting high is not the answer. They've never helped you before. They only mess up your mind and keep you begging for more.

I think of you each day and keep you close to my heart. I feel a loss inside me when we're miles apart.

You're searching for ways to run from the truth. But it will always be behind you. Your lost without direction and don't know which way to turn.

You changed for a while when you said you had Jesus in your life. I thought it was a dream come true and a miracle to save you.

It didn't last long and you were on the run again. Angela, Angela, where are you going now?

Get It Done

I'll dust off all the self-help books that I've put off reading for years.

I'll help someone else who needs a favor or just to get things off their chest.

There are many projects I started but didn't finish. They just laid there to rest.

I'll buy some gourmet coffee and drink in on the porch.

I'll buy a brand new robe and the old one I need to torch.

I'll have my hair colored and cut and my nails long and pink.

I'll light the bathroom with candles and take a long hot bubble bath.

I'll buy me some expensive perfume and diet so I'm not fat.

I want to learn to love myself, too, and stop putting off the things I always wanted to do.

Children

Children are a package of love made forever perfect and sent down from above.

We'll cherish and teach them His name. You give then love and they'll give you the same.

Their smiles are like magic that fills the room with laughter and joy.

They are beautiful baby boys and girls. They'll steal your heart if you give them a chance. All it takes is one little glance.

So be prepared for both the laughter and the tears. If you give them lots of love, it will last for years and years.

What is Life all About?

Turning pages in my mind, I search for answers to the question, "What's life really all about?"

Reaching out from youth until now, I still search for an answer to the question.

Maybe it's not for me to know on this earth . . . how could it, because I've searched my whole life long . . . never feeling I belonged.

On the other side I'll see, maybe find the answers I need. There also will be the love Jesus always promised me. At least I'll find comfort in His arms being free from all harm —- not the pain and tears life was for me here.

I'll help Jesus paint watercolor rainbows after stormy skies.

I'll finally feel joy, no more sorrow in my life. Jesus will lift me up because I know He truly cares. He promised me eternal life in His kingdom to share; if my cross I'll also bear.

Then, I'll finally know the answer to the question; what this life is truly all about. When I take his hand and angels sing on my way to glory land. Yes, I'll help Jesus paint rainbows in colors that fill the sky on the day that Jesus calls me home and I kiss my tears good-by.

A Babe in the Night

Cries from a newborn baby were not heard except by the cold wind that blew through naked trees that sheltered the snow that winter night.

It was by a miracle this little one survived, not knowing her purpose, only that she longed for warmth and love and was denied the blessing and the chance to know a mother's love.

I give thanks to a grandmother I never knew. She gave me the chance to hear a newborn baby cry and the precious and tender love of a mother. But most of all, I thank my own Mother, who gave me life and showed me love. She must have done a wonderful job because, to me, the chance to be a mother is one of the biggest blessings of all.

"For Goodness Sake"

To: The Effingham Police Dept.

I know in my heart my gratitude for the entire Police Dept. and what they do.

They have all worked hard and do their best, to keep us safe and free from harm.

This poem is entwined with care and admiration for the entire police station.

I know they work different shifts and what a toil it must take. Lets help all of them help us "for goodness sake."

They dispatch, patrol, investigate, and arrest. It never ends —- but like the mighty oak, it learns to bend.

I think of all them when it's very early morn. We can sleep safely like a peaceful little baby that is newborn.

They dispatch, patrol, arrest and it never ends. Our town is a beautiful place, but like anywhere; it has its bends.

Of course, they get a little pay for what they do. They go above and beyond the call of duty —- How about you?

It takes more than a day, constantly changing shifts and all that array.

But most of all, they believe in answering the call of enforcing the law, and love the people. This is *Our Hometown* —- called, Effingham, Illinois.

Timothy

Tim is a good-looking fellow. Usually calm and mellow..

He loves to fish and is quite good at it. He's been fishing all his life. His Dad taught him and now he's probably teaching his kid and wife.

He works very hard every day. He does his best and then goes home to rest. I'm sure he's quite tired after putting in a full day. He likes his work and especially the pay.

He has two pit bulls that really look mean, but looks can be deceiving. They're as gentle as a lamb. He takes his dogs for walks, but actually, they take him for a walk.

I wish he'd come by more often. I miss him and the whole family.

Tim's a good guy who treats his family nice.

I'm proud of how Tim turned out to be responsible and caring,

I'm very proud to call Tim my son.

Lean on the Lord

Love is abundant in the heart of our Lord.
He forgives our many sins than loves us even more.
Everyday God is there to hear our many prayers.
He is with you to fight against the devil's many snares.
Lean on God and Jesus, and let them give you strength.
You need to know His love is everlasting and all you need is faith.
God will send His angels to follow you and always keep you safe.
So give a smile to God to show how much you care.
Put all your love and trust in Him —- He isn't going anywhere.

Dedicated to My Sis, Precious Patty

In the twilight hours I look up into the heaven and the stars and thank the Lord for all my blessings He has given me so far.

I wipe tears and bow my head to pray and ask Jesus to help me make the sorrow and pain go away.

I look forward to heaven and the peace there I will find. Everlasting joy it is promised, will be mine.

Dedicated to James Dillow

I am a police officer. Most people call me a cop. I say a prayer each morning when my son says, "See you Pop."

I never know what circumstances I will have to face when I answer a call sometimes it's a total rat race.

I try each day to help preserve the laws and freedom in this God given land.

I love my job, but sometimes the stress, it's more than I can stand.

Then there is a wreck and I saved someone's life. I realize then, she's someone's mother or young wife.

I thank God for the courage and dedication I take with me as I back up from my house. But, I'm an American with honor. That's what it meant to me.

Reona is Her Name

She's very special and her *dangled* feel the same.

She has a heart of gold and will share her love with many until she's very old. Reona is a beautiful name and she suits her name well.

I will always remember Reona, her caring and sweet voice. She goes beyond the call of duty if she knows someone needs help. She cares. Reona, thank you for all you've done for me.

May God bless you ten fold and so happy He'll help you be.

May all your dreams come true because there's no one as sweet and special as you… I will never forget how sweet you were to me.

Enjoy Each Day

Our lives go by so very fast and today will soon pass, so very fast.

Tomorrow is just a word we know; but it may not come to pass.

So make the best and enjoy what you have, love others and show them you care. If you are blessed, take the time to always share.

There are so many things we don't take the time to enjoy. Hug your sweet grandchildren, either a pretty little girl or boy. They'll be grown before we know it.

Watch the sunrise with someone you love and watch the colors turn from purple and orange to soft pale pink and glow. Buy yourself a single gorgeous, perfect yellow rose and enjoy its fragrance with your cute little freckled nose.

Embrace life and praise God for being there in both times of joy and times of strife.

Live each day like it's your last, and before long, the day will pass.

Someday we'll pass on to a place called glory land and I'm going to try my best to make it there. If I follow God's guidance, I know I can.

Today I'm going to embrace and love the day. I know God is with me and I'll be with Him also someday.

Crossroads Bank

There are many banks in Effingham; but in all of our hometown not a better one can be found like Crossroads Bank.

Crossroads Bank has been my bank for years and I found it to be the best bank all around.

They greet you with a beautiful smile and appreciate their customers. Their service is number one.

I love the dignity and respect the bank gives to everyone who comes through their doors.

So, do your banking at a number one bank and you will be glad you did.

No other bank even comes close, and I know this from my own experience.

When I have business to take care of, it's through their doors I go.

So, come on in for some fresh coffee and see for yourself how much they care.

Come to a place that appreciates each customer they deal with.

You'll be glad you did.

My Sweet Sister, Linda

I am very blessed to have a sister who not only tells me she loves me, but shows me, too.

When I talk to her it makes my day because she makes me laugh and is very wise and always knows just what to do and say. She's full of wisdom and common sense and I trust her all the way.

She has so many talents. I don't know where to begin; but best of all my sister Linda knows how to be a good friend.

When I need to share something she listens and really cares. She gives me her time and is always kind.

It's hard for me to believe sometimes all the strength and courage that this sweet sister has, but I do know she has a very strong faith.

She's endured a lot of challenges and pain, but still stays calm and her good judgment remains. I can trust her with whatever I say and know just with her it will stay.

I am blessed and I love the time we spend together.

She's fun and witty and I can always be myself when I'm with her. My memories of Linda, I will cherish forever until the very end. I love and admire her for what she's accomplished in her life.

She's a great mother, grandmother, and wife. She keeps a beautiful home and enjoys life. She's also a great sister and may God bless her in every way and may happiness be hers each and every single day.

An Angel that We Know

Dotty was a true inspiration and adored by all who knew her well.

She loved life when she when she was well and in her sparkling eyes you could tell.

She was a true gift to know and you couldn't help but lover her so.

If you had the honor to be her friend, then this you would know.

When she was well, you could tell how much respect she had for others.

Dotty was a great and fascinating gift from God; and Him, she knew well.

She always thought of others and was a wonderful mother, wife and friend.

She hung on as long as she could. Jack took care of her to the very end. He loved her so.

A woman dedicated as a friend, she touched the lives and hearts of many. She was always taking the time to help others . . . There was no end to the way she would give.

We feel a great loss because they'll never be a person more divine than she.

Now she is with Jesus and she suffers no more. Jack was and is a loving and devoted friend and husband.

I don't think Dotty wants us to mourn, but to remember the happy times.

When she was happy and healthy, her friendship was etched inside our hearts.

So, let's do what I think she would want us to do and remember all the good and happy times.

Now Dotty has peace and rest and she is smiling down upon us.

Of all the great people I ever knew, Dotty is at the very top of the list. We will remember you forever.

With sincere respect and love from,

Leona Faye Horath
January 18, 2012

Faith Will Carry You Through

When your days are dark and bleak and you're so sad you cannot speak, just remember that Jesus is there. He never went anywhere. We all have bad times when we want to give up, but remember to let faith carry you through.

Jesus cries for you and He also feels your pain. He'll be there with you in both the bright sunshine and the dark and cold rain.

When all your friends turn their back on you and you don't know who you can turn to, lean on Jesus and let faith carry you through.

Love

Love is just a word until you really feel it in your heart. I fell in love with you, sweetheart from the very start. You have made my dreams come true. I've always wanted someone just like you. I want you to know I will always love you and hope forever you will love me, too.

The Eagle

To a man who has given his all.

Whatever the need is, he answers the call.

He is such a blessing to know. He is powered by sheer faith and it shows.

He is one of a kind with a big heart and sharp mind. He gives his all and is there when you fall.

I have deep respect for a man named, John Monnet, who can't seem to do enough. He's tender, yet he's tough. I can't begin to tell you how he keeps on going went the road is rough.

God smiles at the mention of his name. He wants to do good for everyone and doesn't care about power or fame.

I have the pleasure to give him a gift that he'll treasure forever and will make him smile.

When he needs a lift, John Monnet is an Eagle who flies above the clouds. It's an honor to know him, and because he's such a fine man and sheriff, we are very proud. He doesn't soar alone, God is with him today and forever more . . .The Eagle that soars alone.

Clyde's Dream

Many years ago Clyde Martin had a dream to own a grocery store in a good ole' small town called, Effingham, Illinois.

Clyde knew it would take a lot of work, but sheer belief and dedication was all it took, plus a lot of faith was what he had.

He treated his customers well and everyone began to tell of the great service they received along with the sales that others couldn't compete.

Years went by and Clyde had a dream in his eye, because his dream came true and his family became part of it, too.

He kept building on and making the parking lot and store bigger and still the store was full of people. Bargains and great service was the Martin tool.

Not only did Clyde's dream come true, but the people of Effingham loved and admired him, too. Martin's is now a super store that spreads over a block or more!

Clyde passed on to heaven years ago and his wonderful son, Newlin, runs the whole show.

Still, the giant parking lot is always full and you're greeted with a smile from all the employees who always stay there a long while.

I'm proud of the Martin family who are almost a legend in our town.

Clyde knew in his heart, with a lot of work and dedication, he would take off from the start.

I myself remember Clyde and the positive attitude he had. Even as a small child, he was always kind and mild.

So here's to you Clyde Martin and the dream you made come true; and here's a cheer to Newlin and all his dedicated employees who carry on.

Dealing with Crime

Today is a new day I have to face with problems and prejudice I can't erase.

I have to deal with crime, but it's just a matter of time when they'll get caught even though they fought there going down.

I give each day my all and respond to every call with dignity and respect. There's a lot to deal with, but I fact the day and give it all I got.

I'm a cop and I fight crime, protect and served every minute of the hour. God gives me strength and power and I'll do my best and I won't rest until my shift is over.

I want to go home with my wife and kids, but first let me catch the bad guys and put them behind bars.

Drugs and dealing, vandalism and steeling and it's usually the same faces. We book them and put them in jail. They'll make bail and walk the streets, and once again, they'll meet the dirty scum that gets them on drugs in the first place.

So, I do my best and it won't let me rest and I won't back down or cover.

God gives me the strength and power. I want safe streets for my kids. So, lets put back on the lid, gain control, and make them run.

I want the beauty we once had. So, lets get rid of crime so your kids can play safe in the streets of their hometown.

CPSIA information can be obtained
at www.ICGtesting.com
Printed in the USA
LVHW050214281021
701764LV00011B/210

9 781480 967830